How to Draw Dragons Step by Step - Volume 2 - (Step by step instructions on how to draw dragons)

This book has over 300 detailed illustrations that demonstrate how to draw dragons step by step

J.P. Manning

21. Adjusting the pressure you place
on your pencil will help you vary the
thickness of your lines.

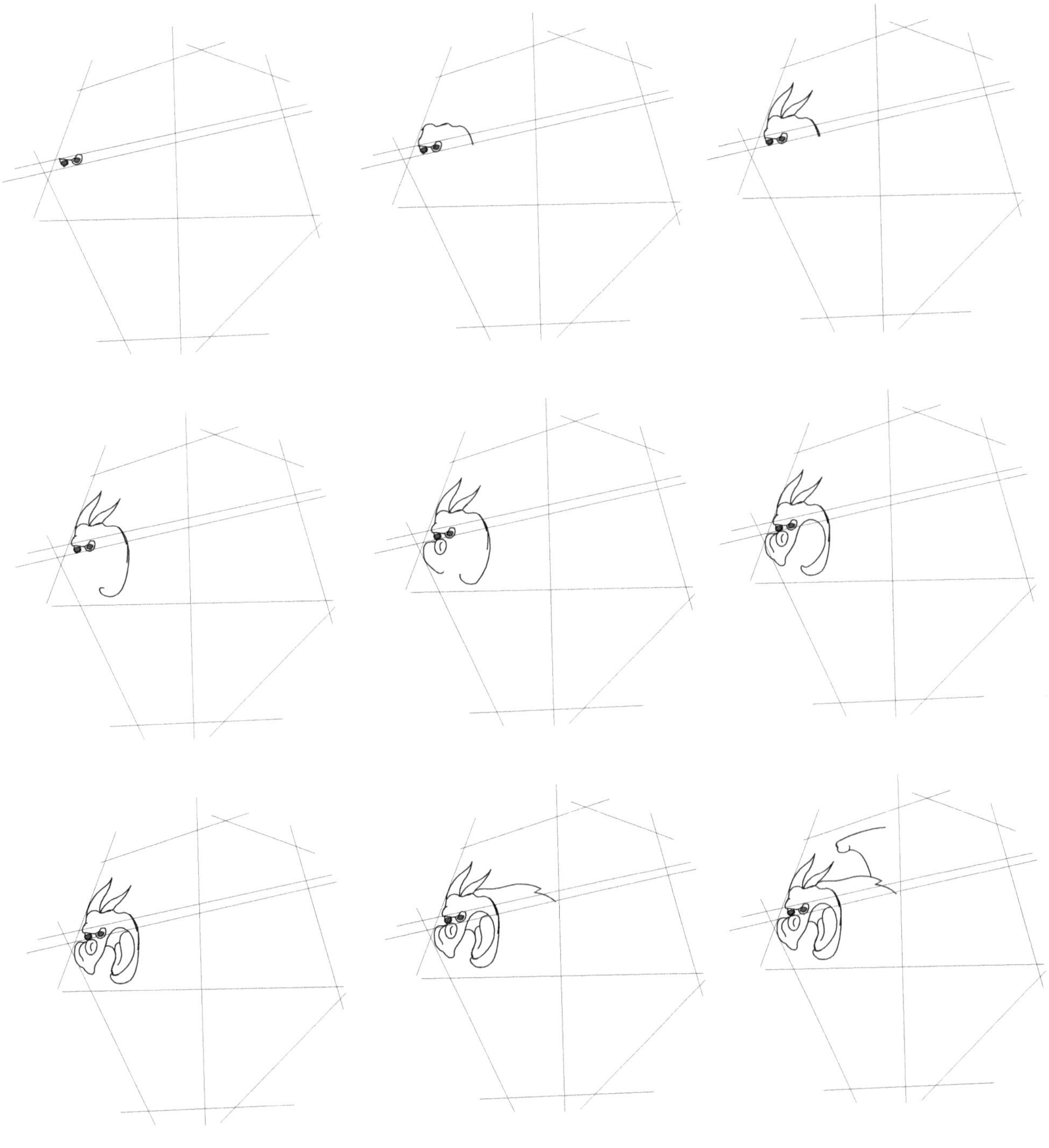

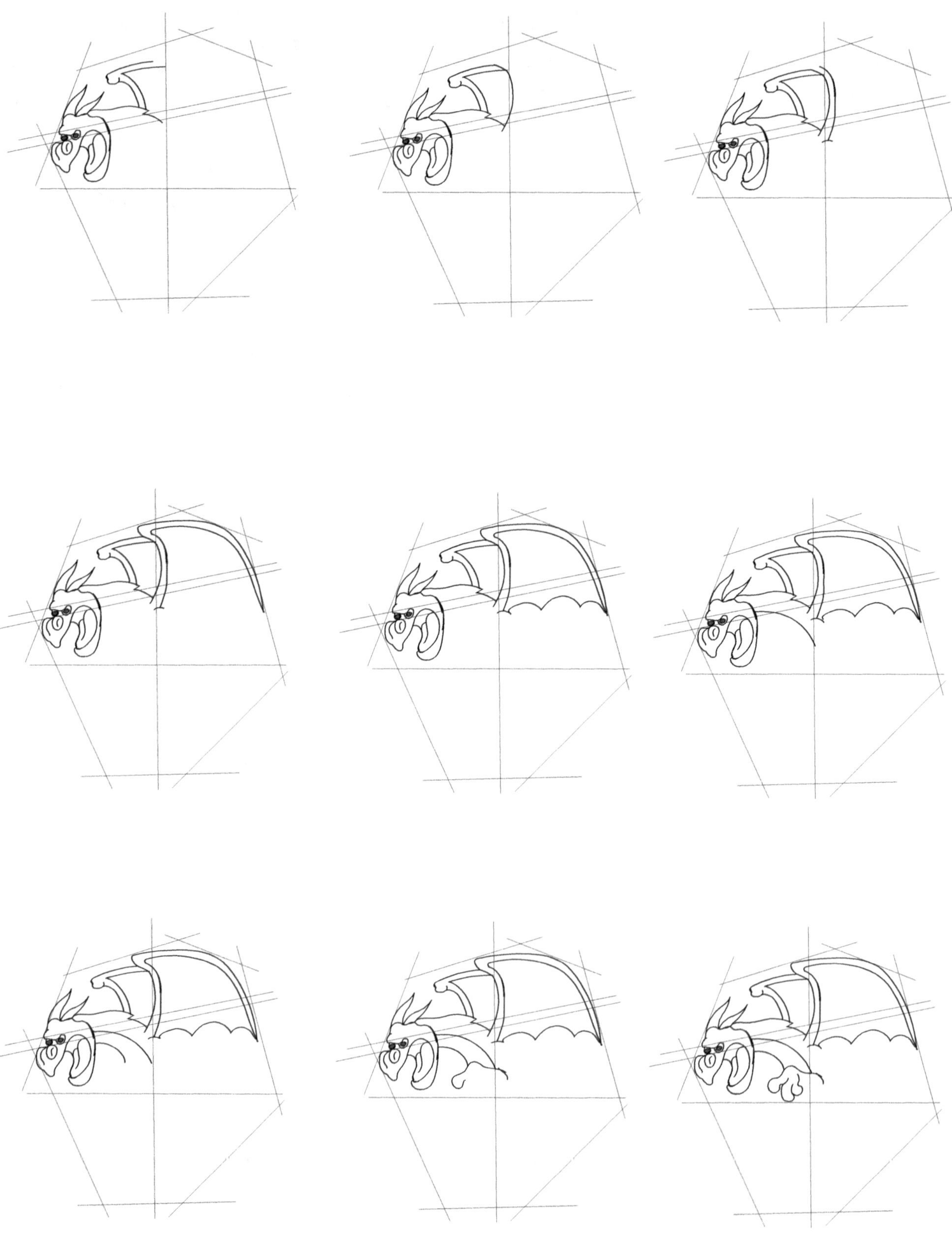

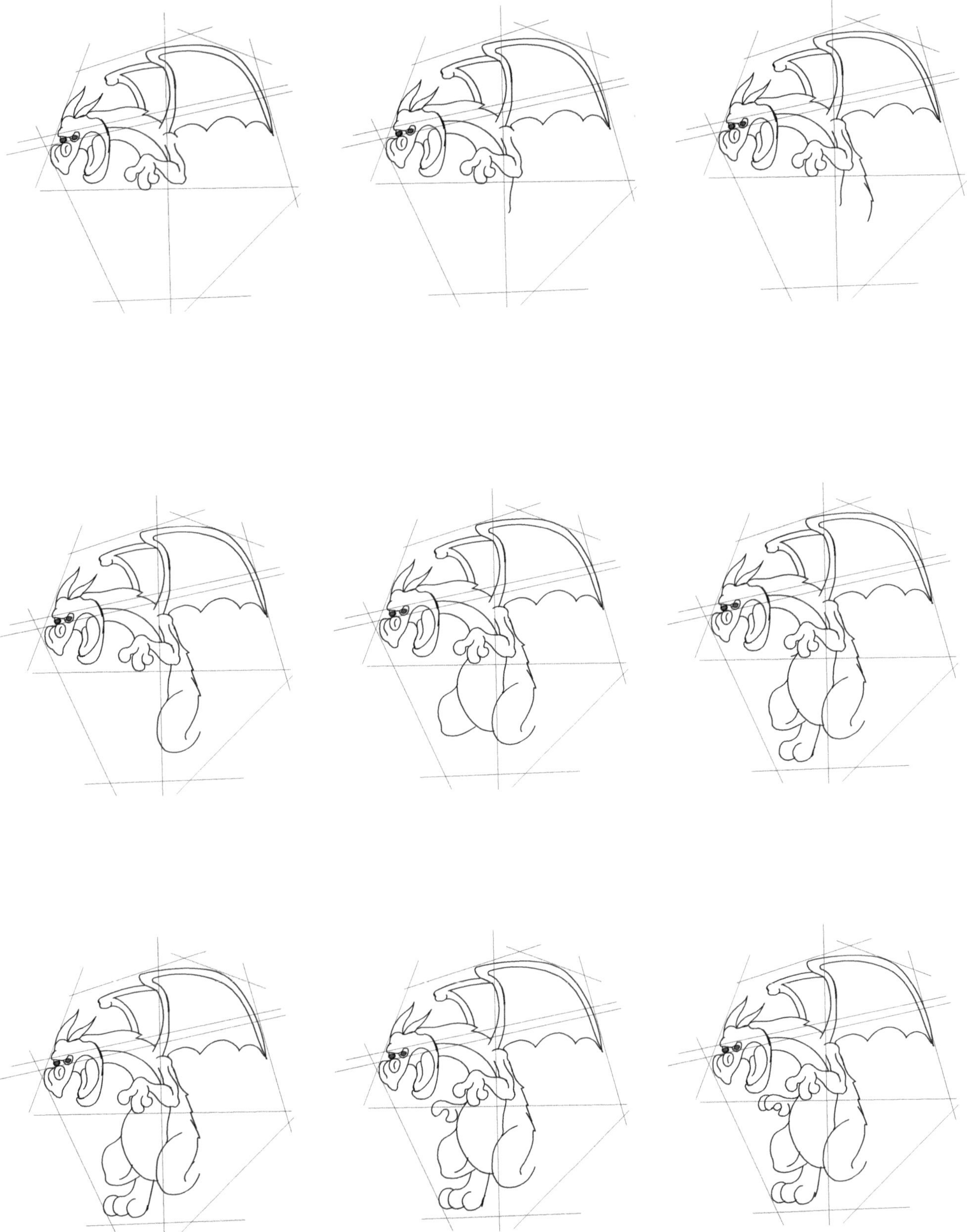

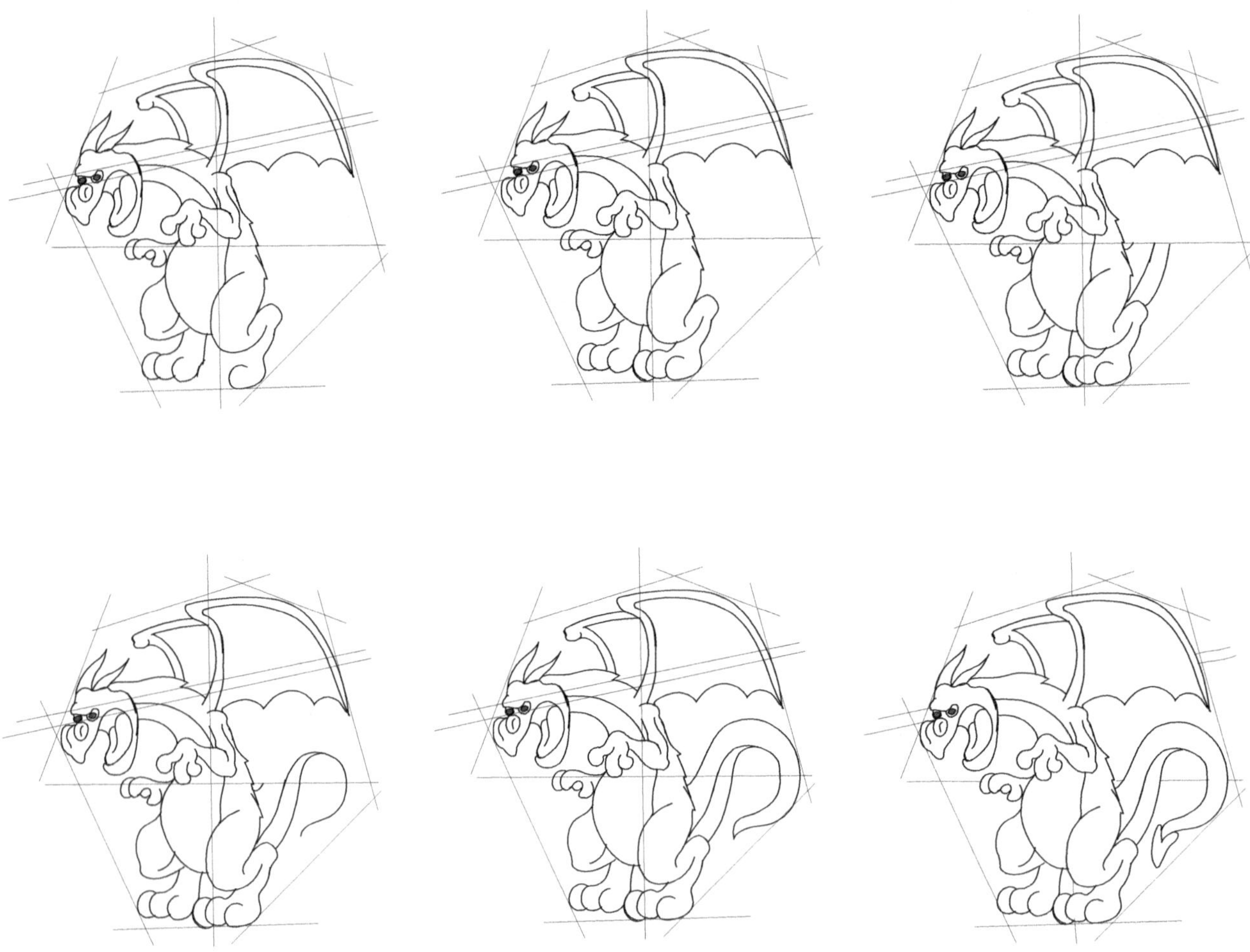

Dragons are legendary creatures that appear in the folklore of many cultures worldwide, spanning continents and civilizations. In Chinese mythology, dragons are revered as benevolent and powerful beings, symbolizing strength, prosperity, and good fortune. They are often depicted as serpentine creatures with long bodiesand four legs, capable of controlling water and weather.

22. After you have drawn your character's head it is easier to add small details.

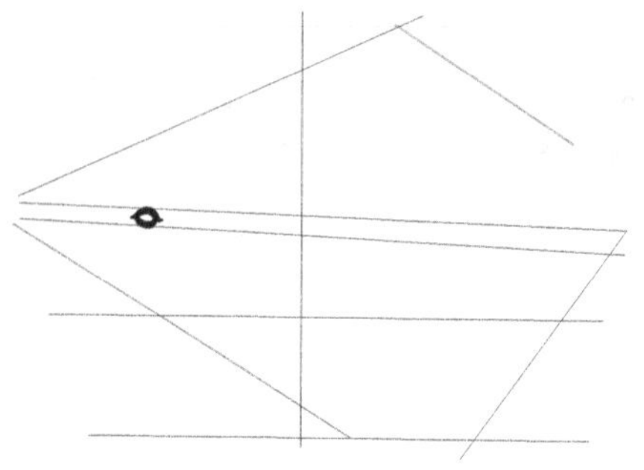

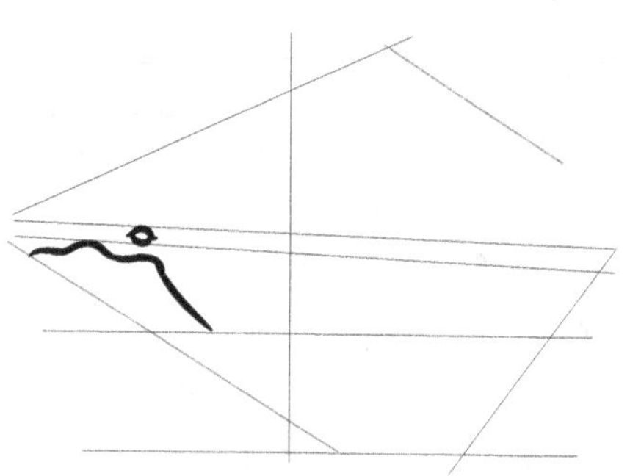

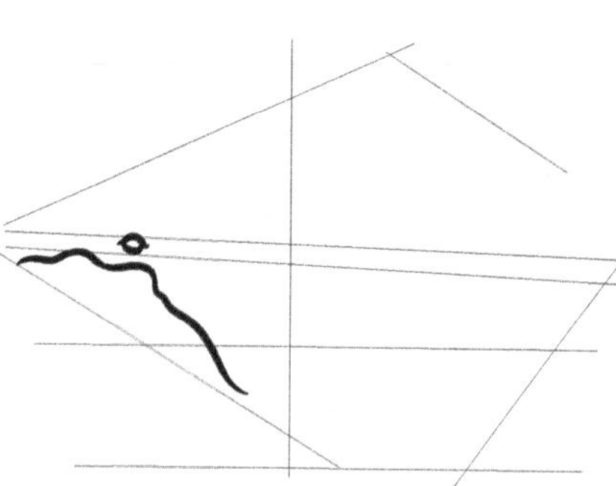

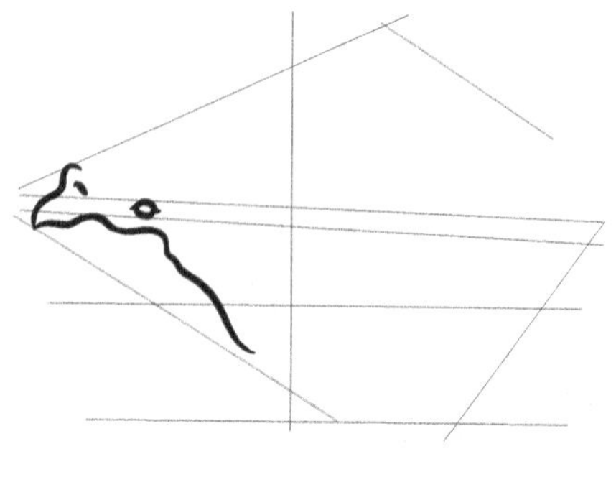

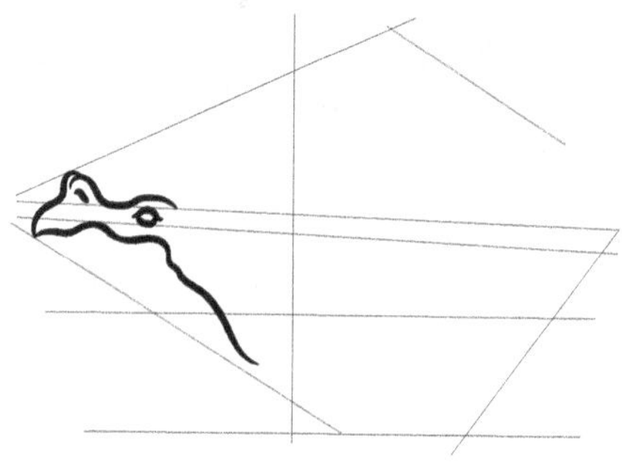

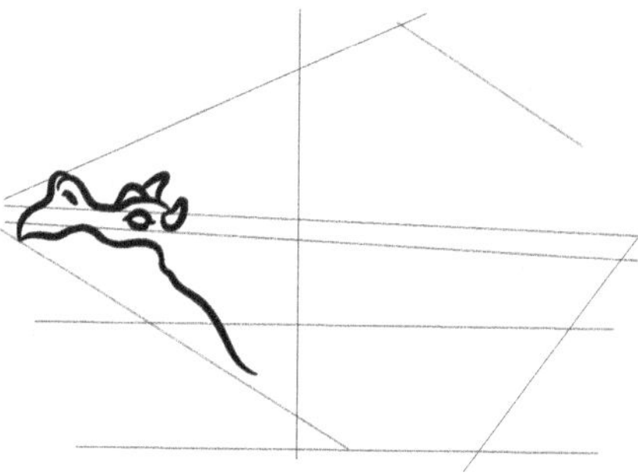

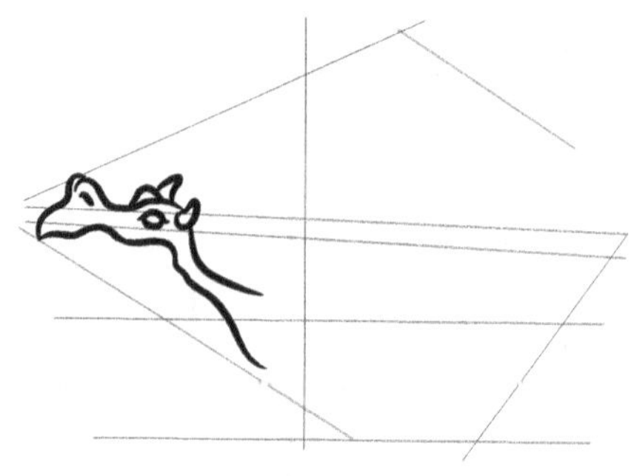

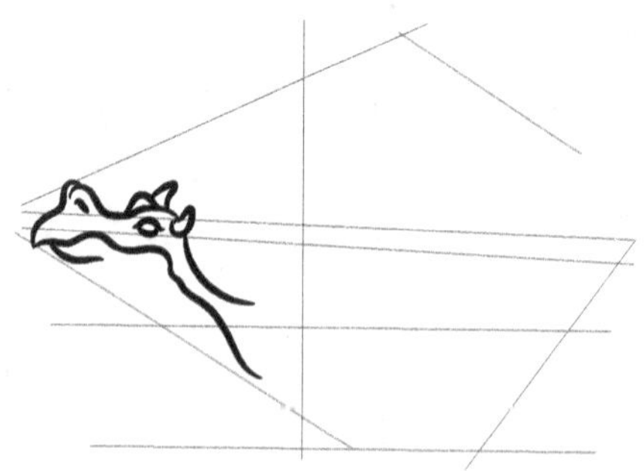

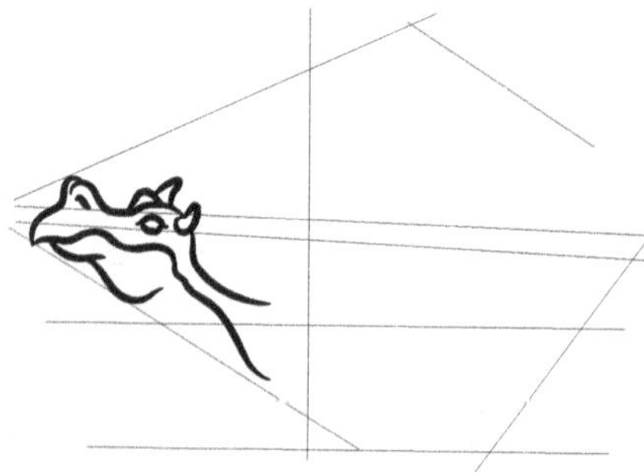

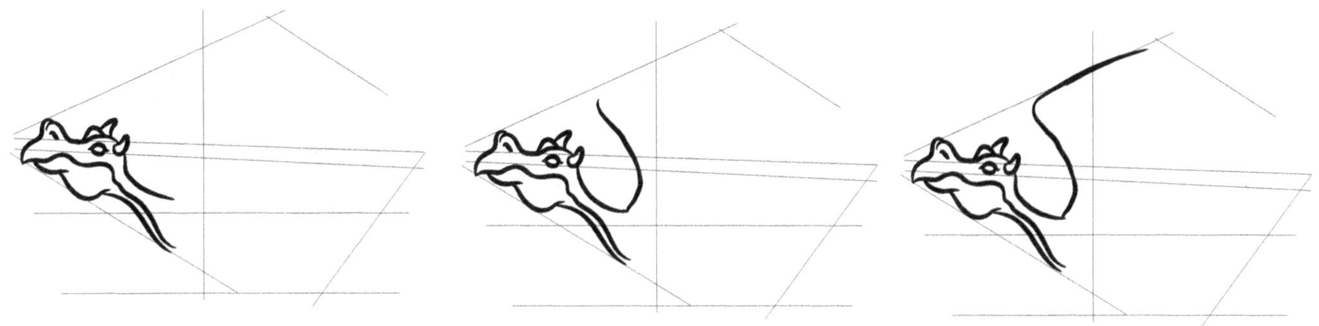

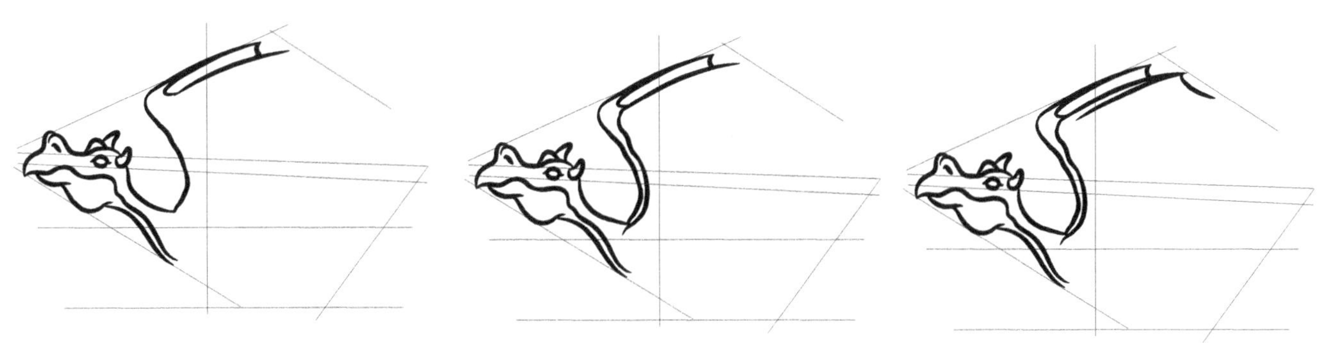

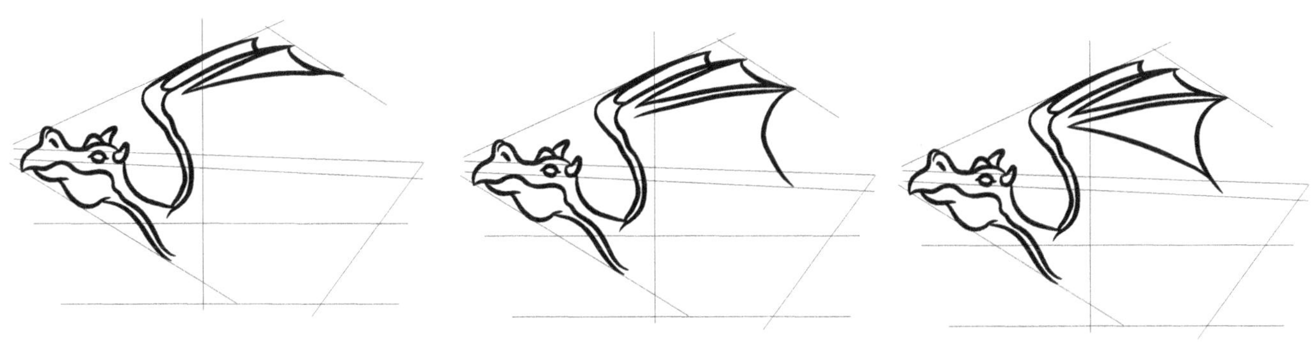

In Western cultures, dragons often represent chaos and evil. They are typically portrayed as fearsome, fire-breathing creatures that hoard treasure and wreak havoc. Western dragons are frequently the antagonists in tales of heroism and adventure, embodying danger and destruction. This dragon is having a carefree moment.

23. Separate your grid into sections
to help you decide how you want
to proportion your drawing. This
can help you to alter the height of
your character.

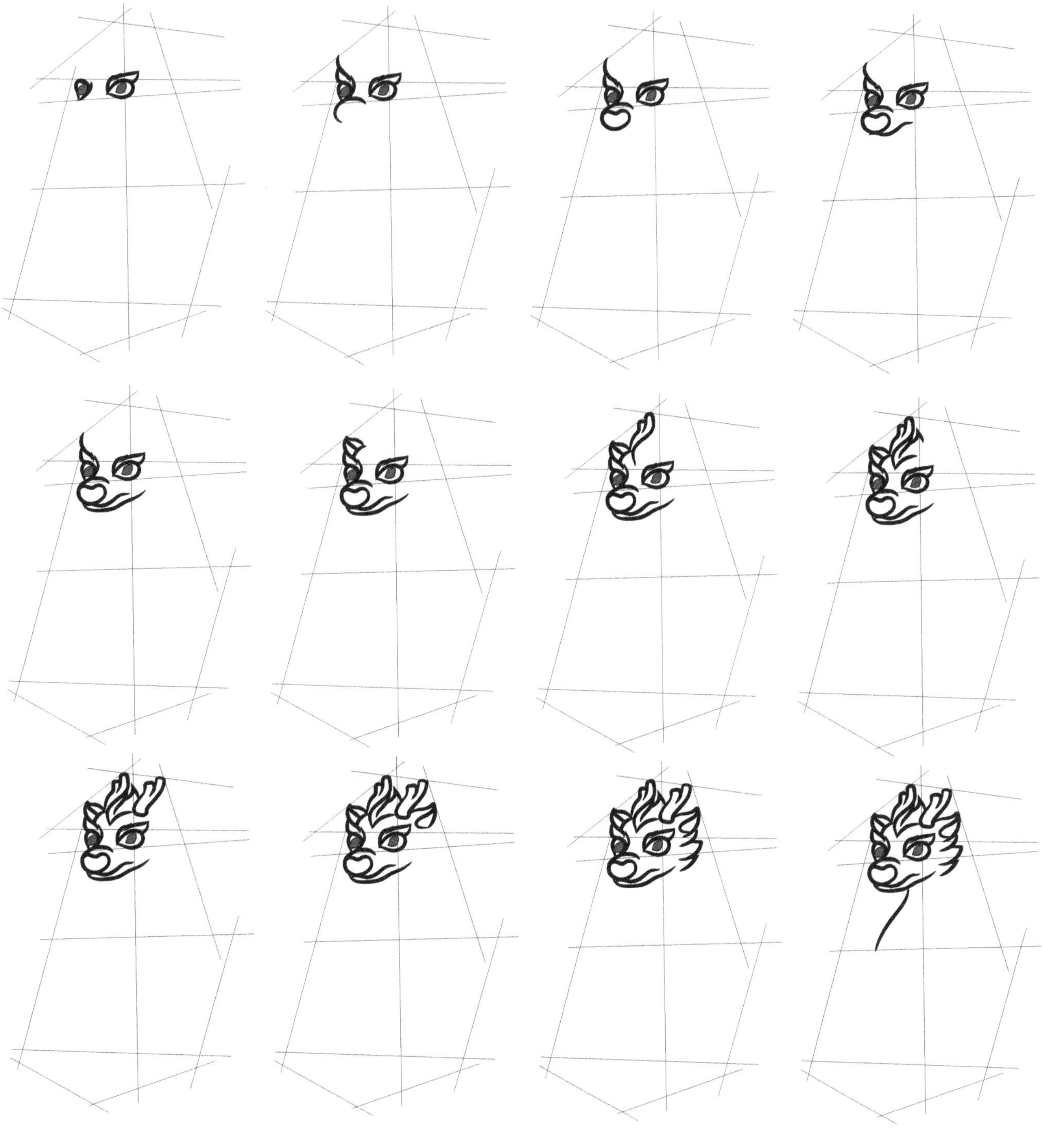

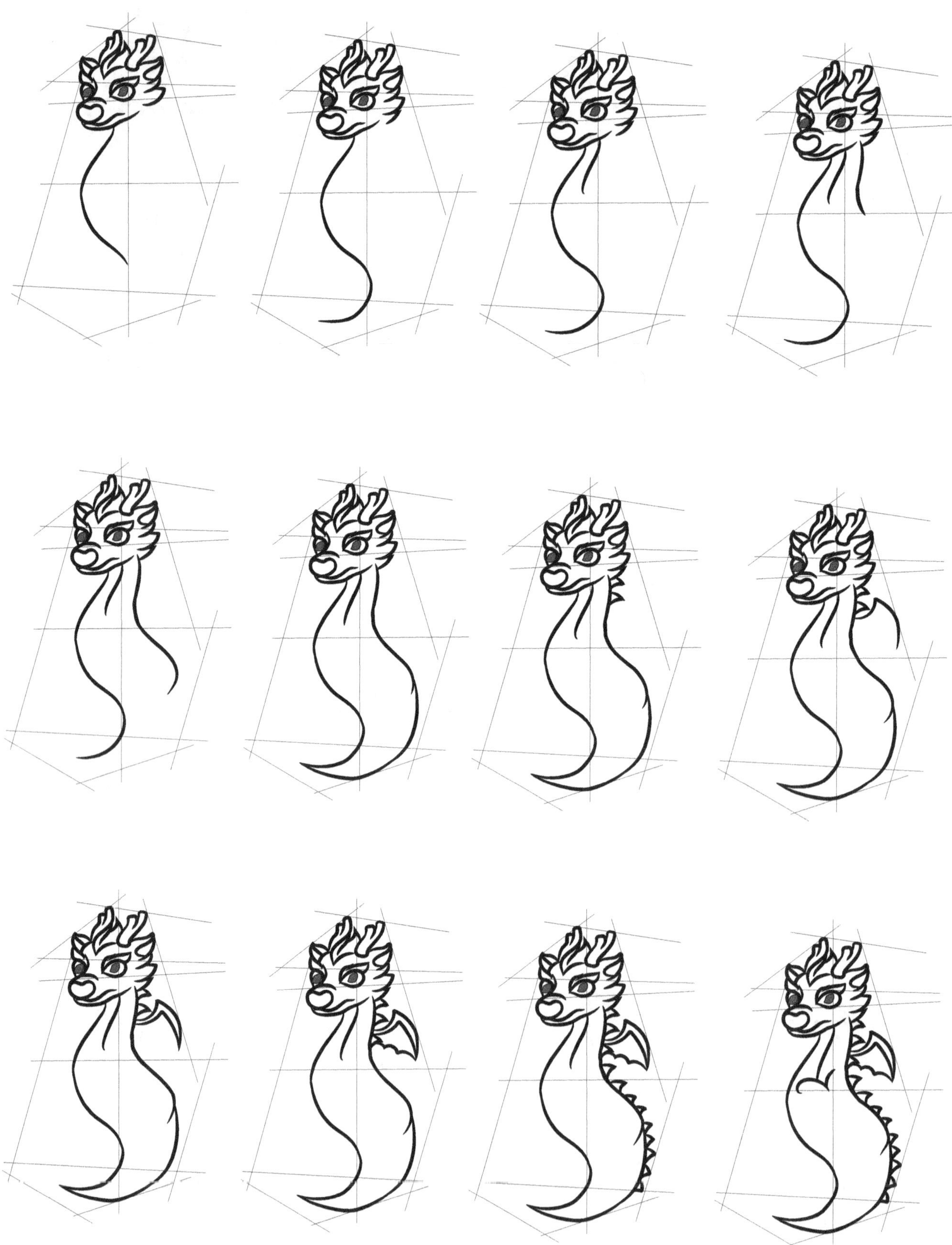

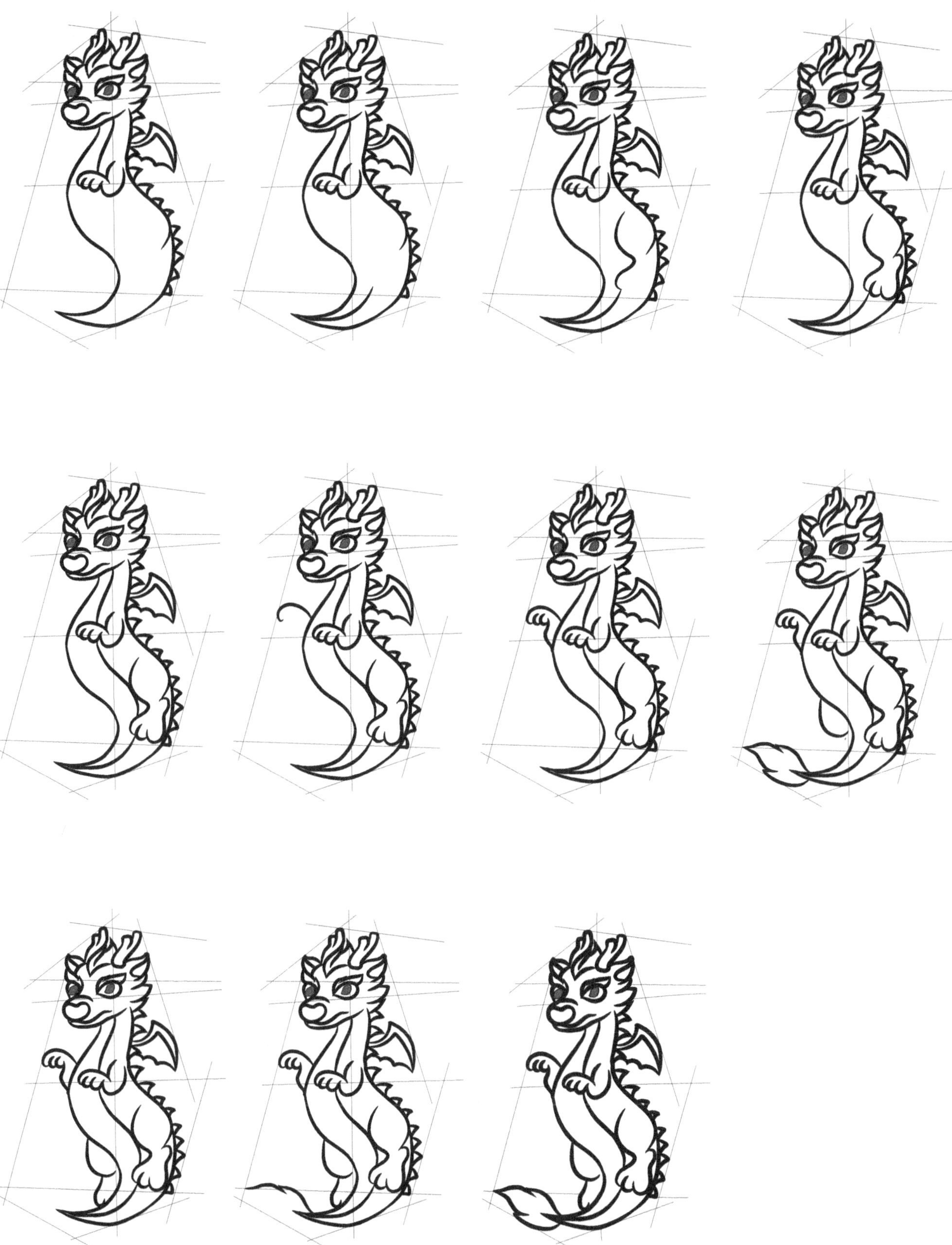

A horned-back dragon typically has a series of large, bony protrusions or spikes running down its spine, starting from the top of its head and continuing along its back to the tip of its tail. These horns can vary in size and shape, with some being short and curved, while others are long and jagged. The scales of the dragon are usually tough and resilient, often depicted in dark, earthy tones such as deep green, black, or dark brown. Varying the size of your dragon's norns can make them look more unique.

24. You can make your character more original by exaggerating some of its features.

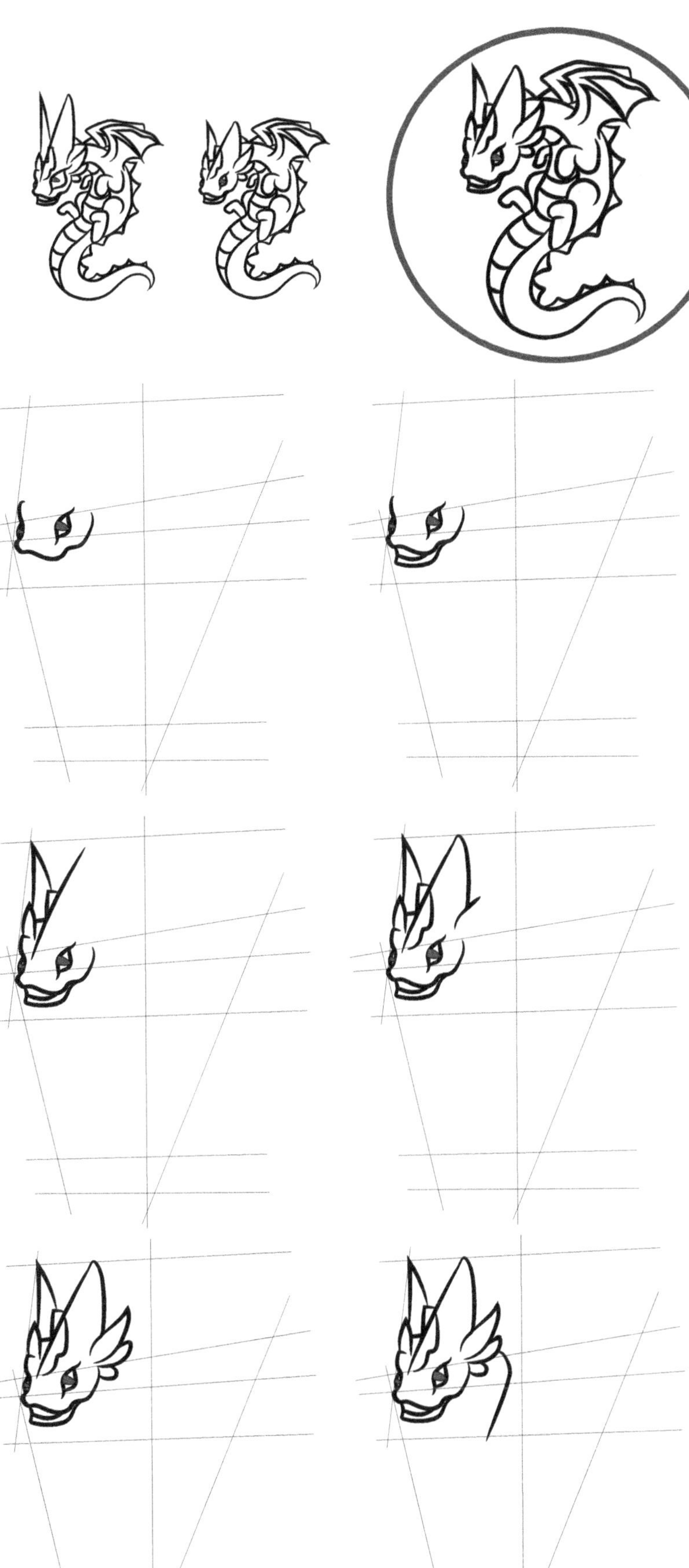

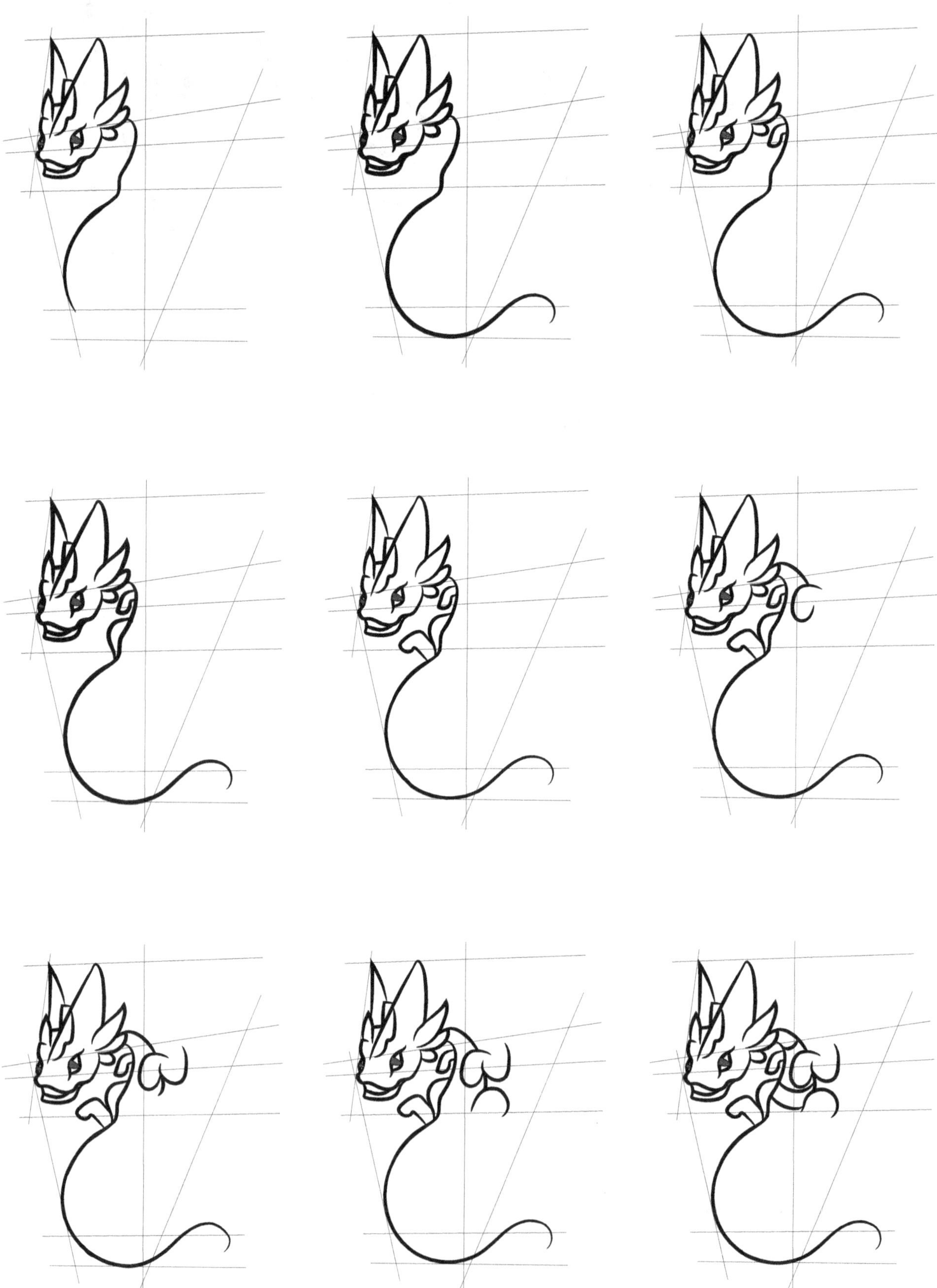

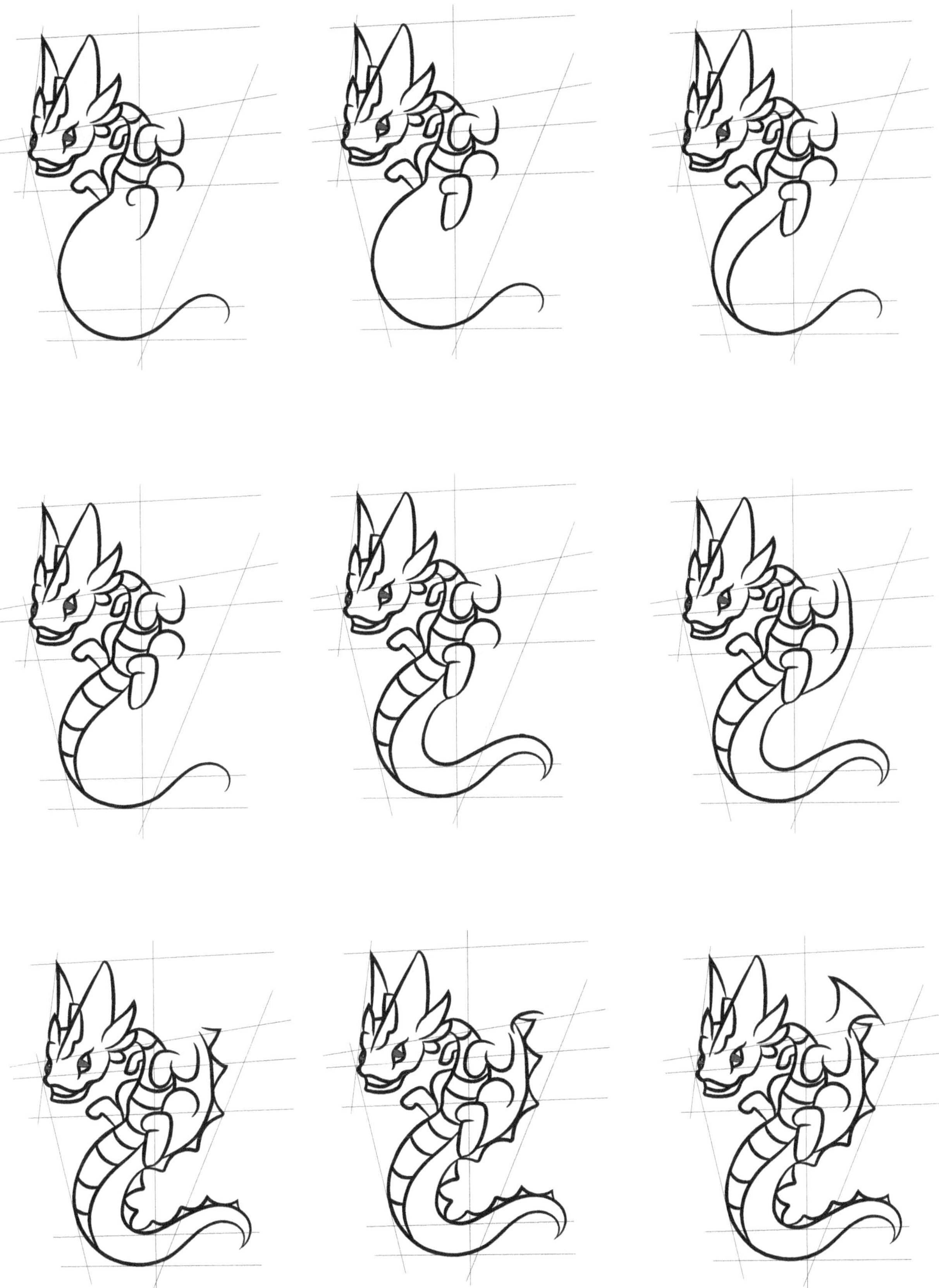

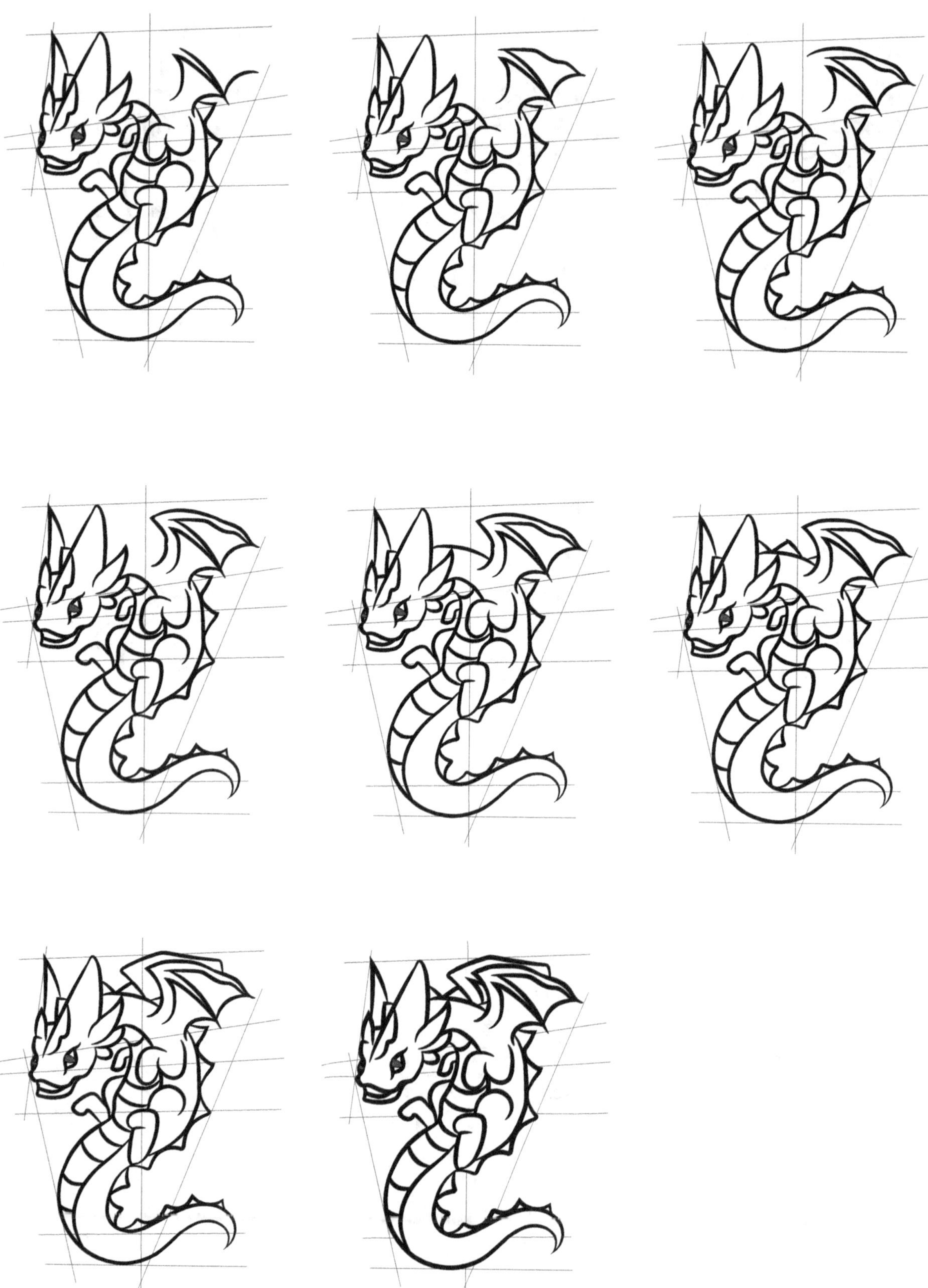

Dragons with long, serpentine bodies are particularly prominent in East Asian mythology, especially within Chinese, Japanese, and Korean cultures. These dragons, often called "lung" in Chinese or "ryū" in Japanese, differ significantly from their Western counterparts, which are typically depicted with stockier, more lizard-like physiques. Vary the length of your dragon's body to make it look more unique.

25. Enlarging the eyes of your characters can make them look more childlike.

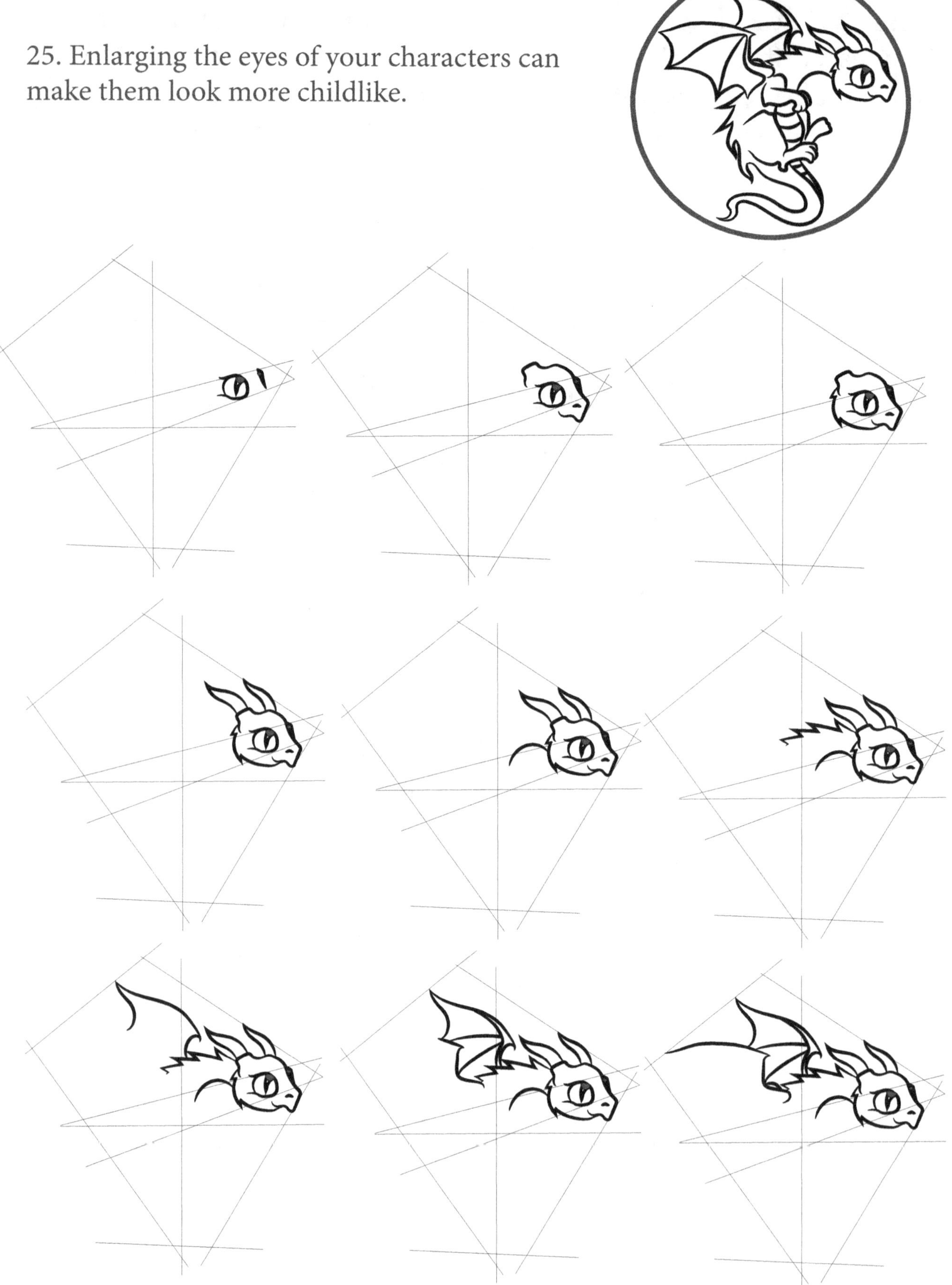

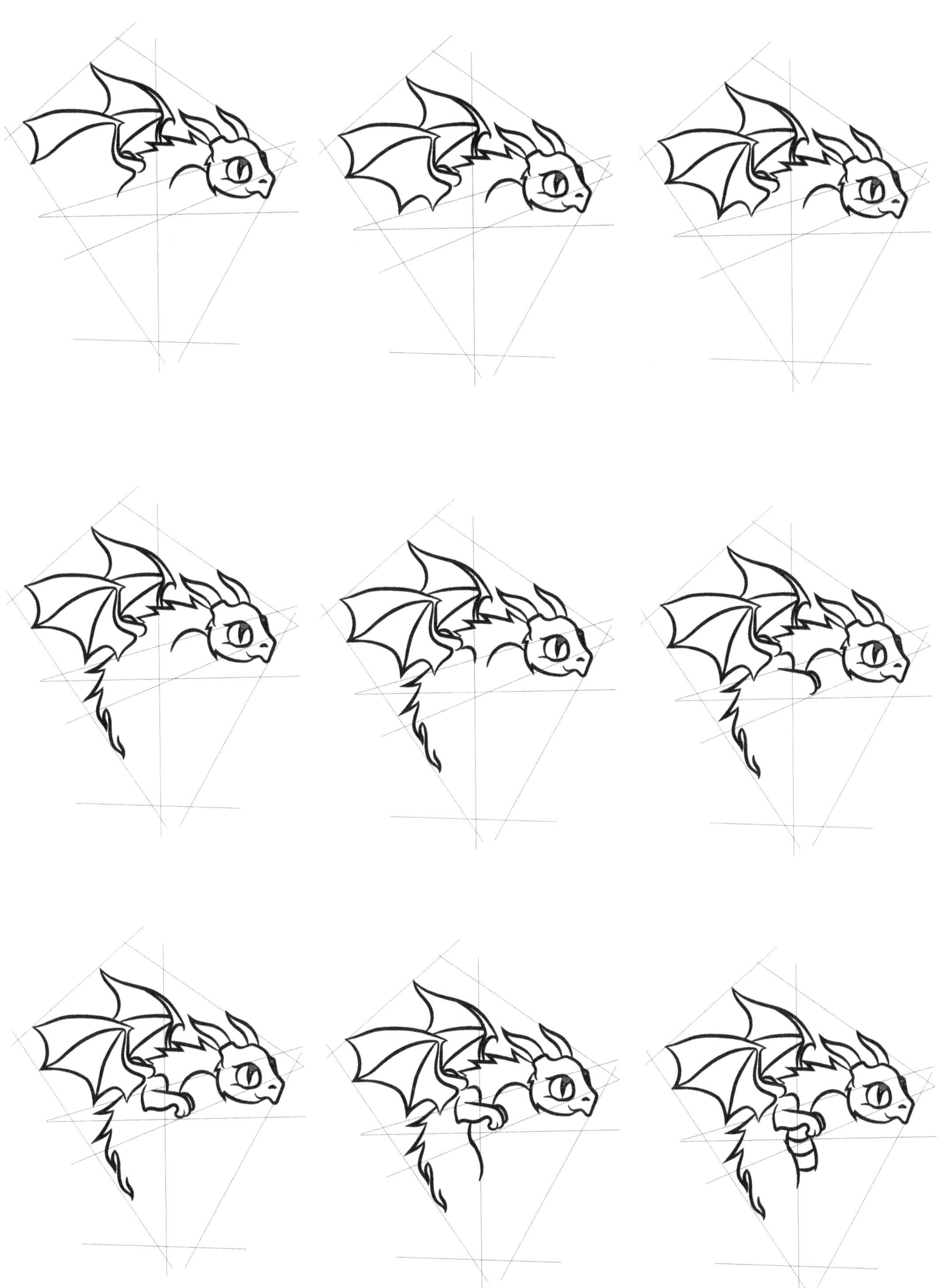

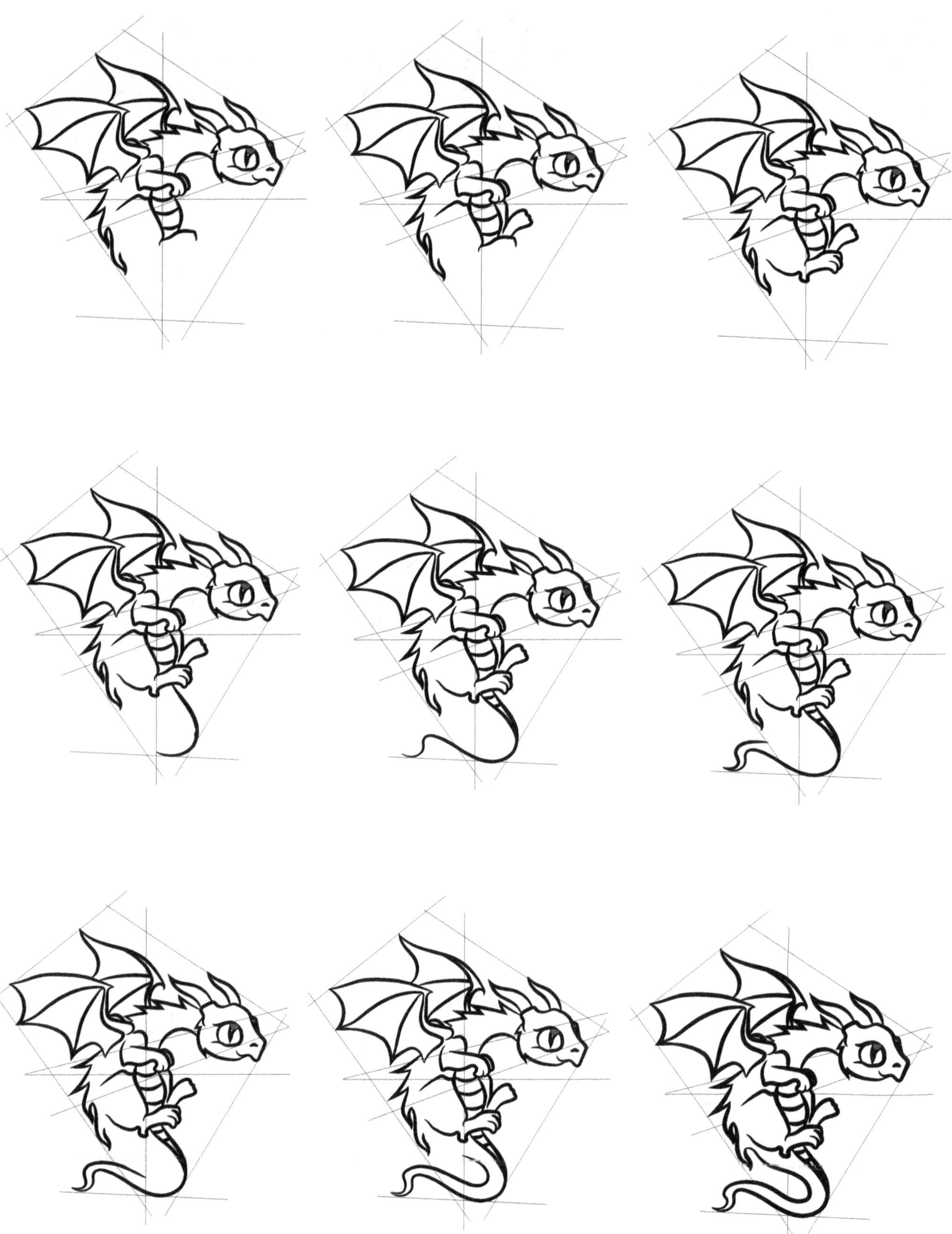

Making your dragon's eyes smaller could make it appear very different

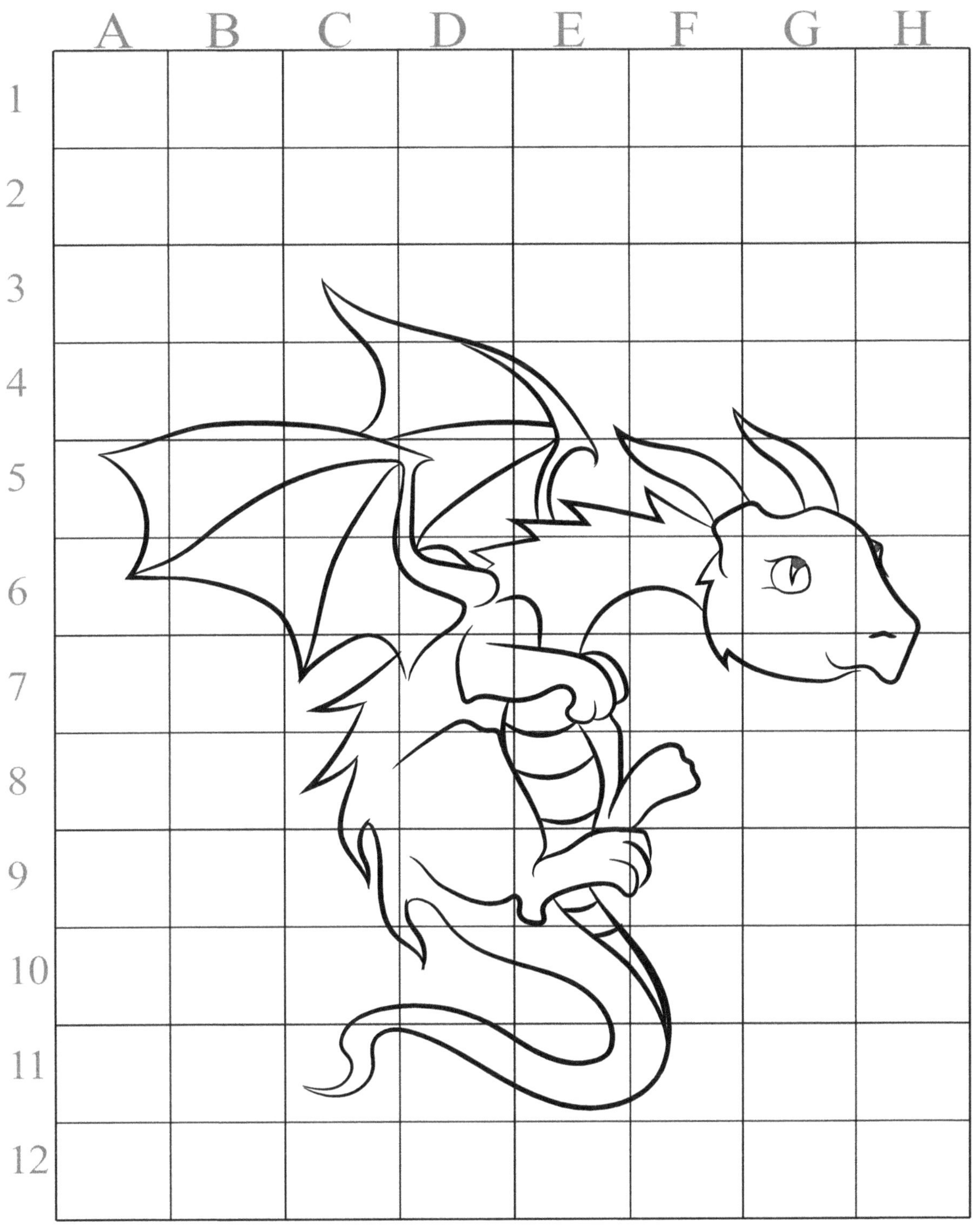

26. The use of ellipses in your grid can bring roundness into your drawing.

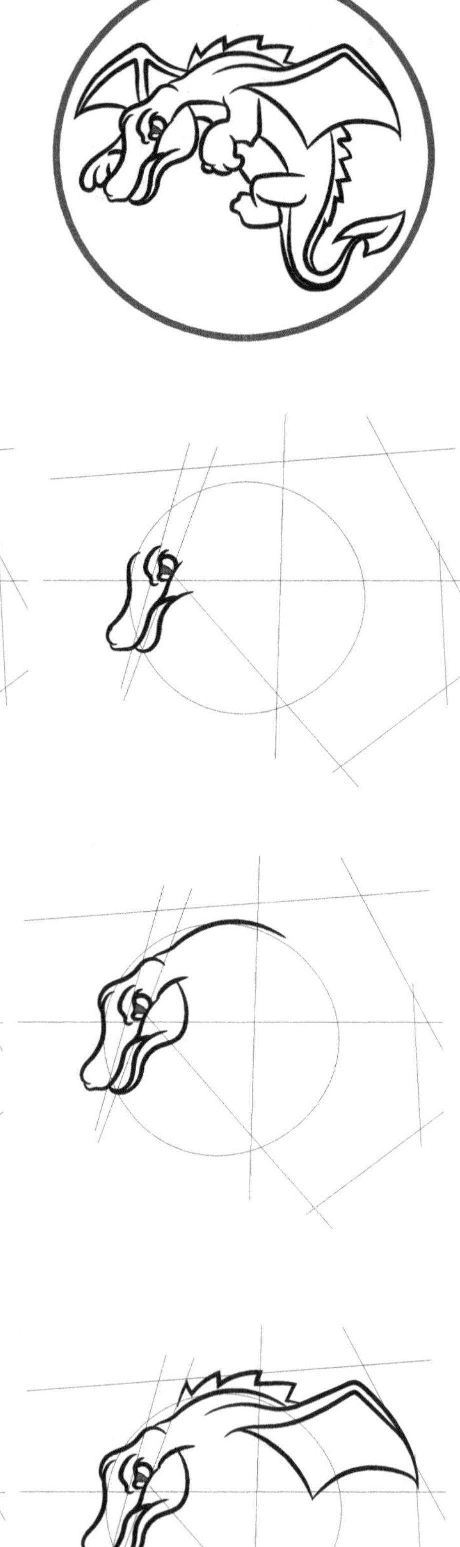

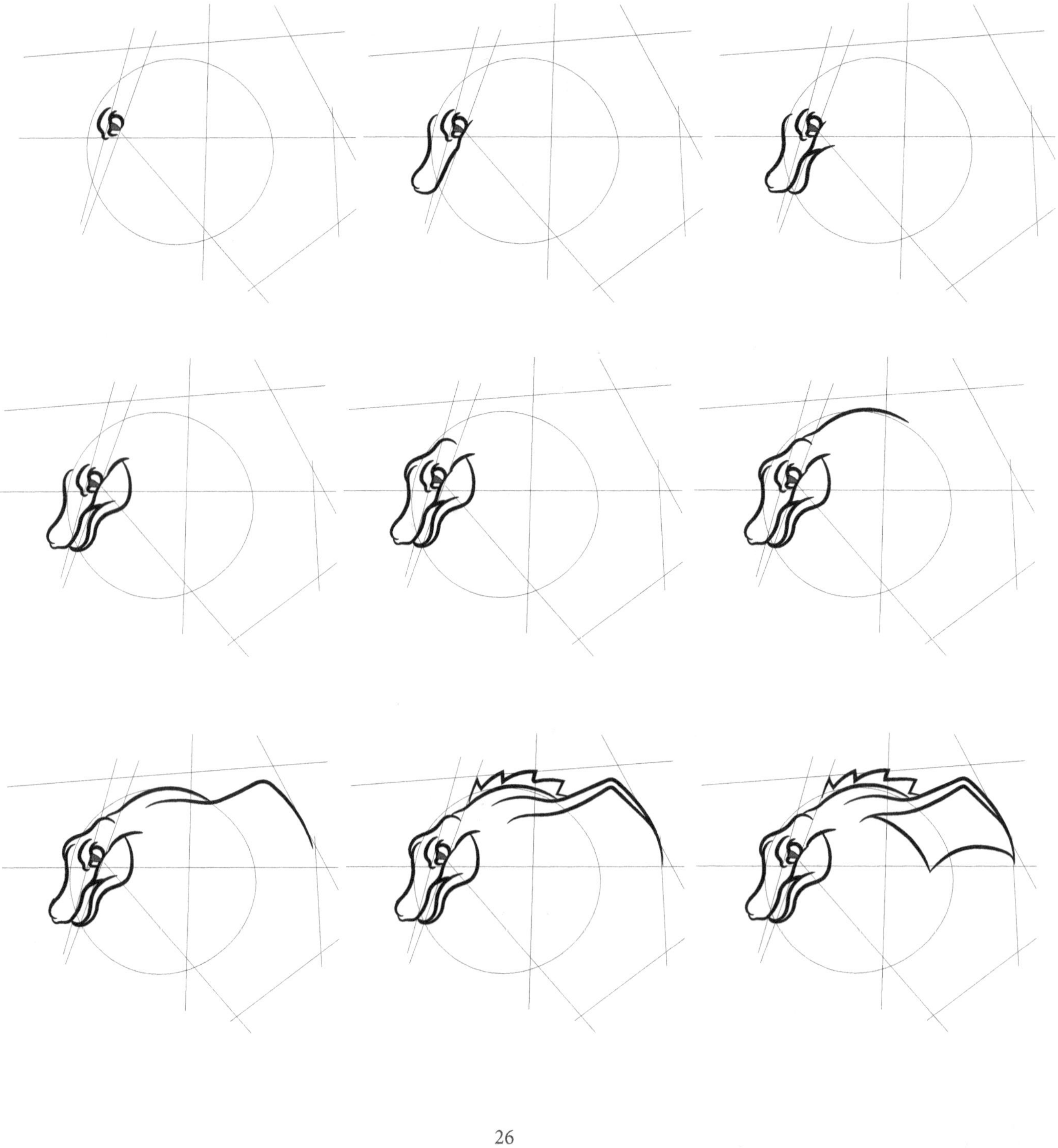

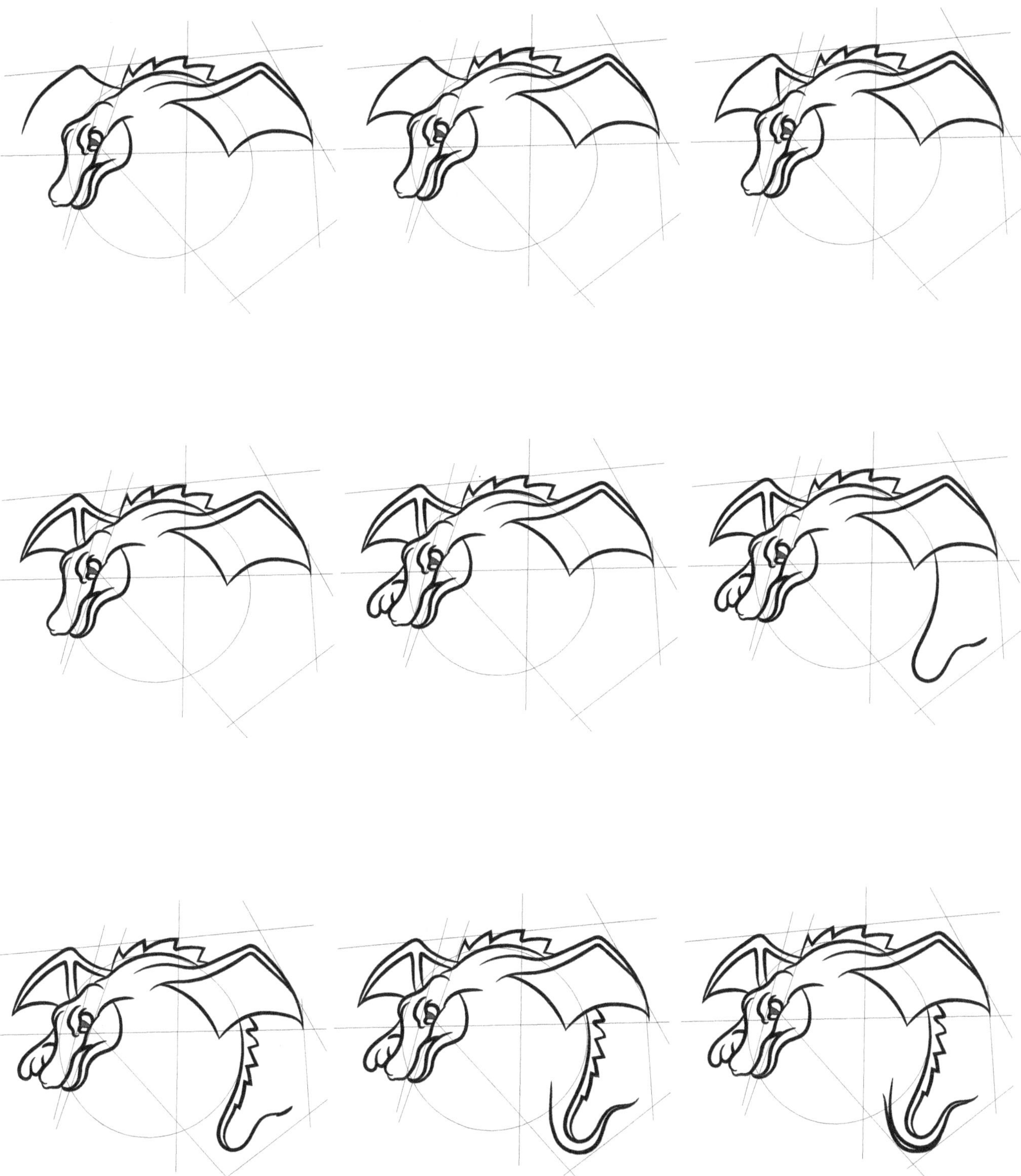

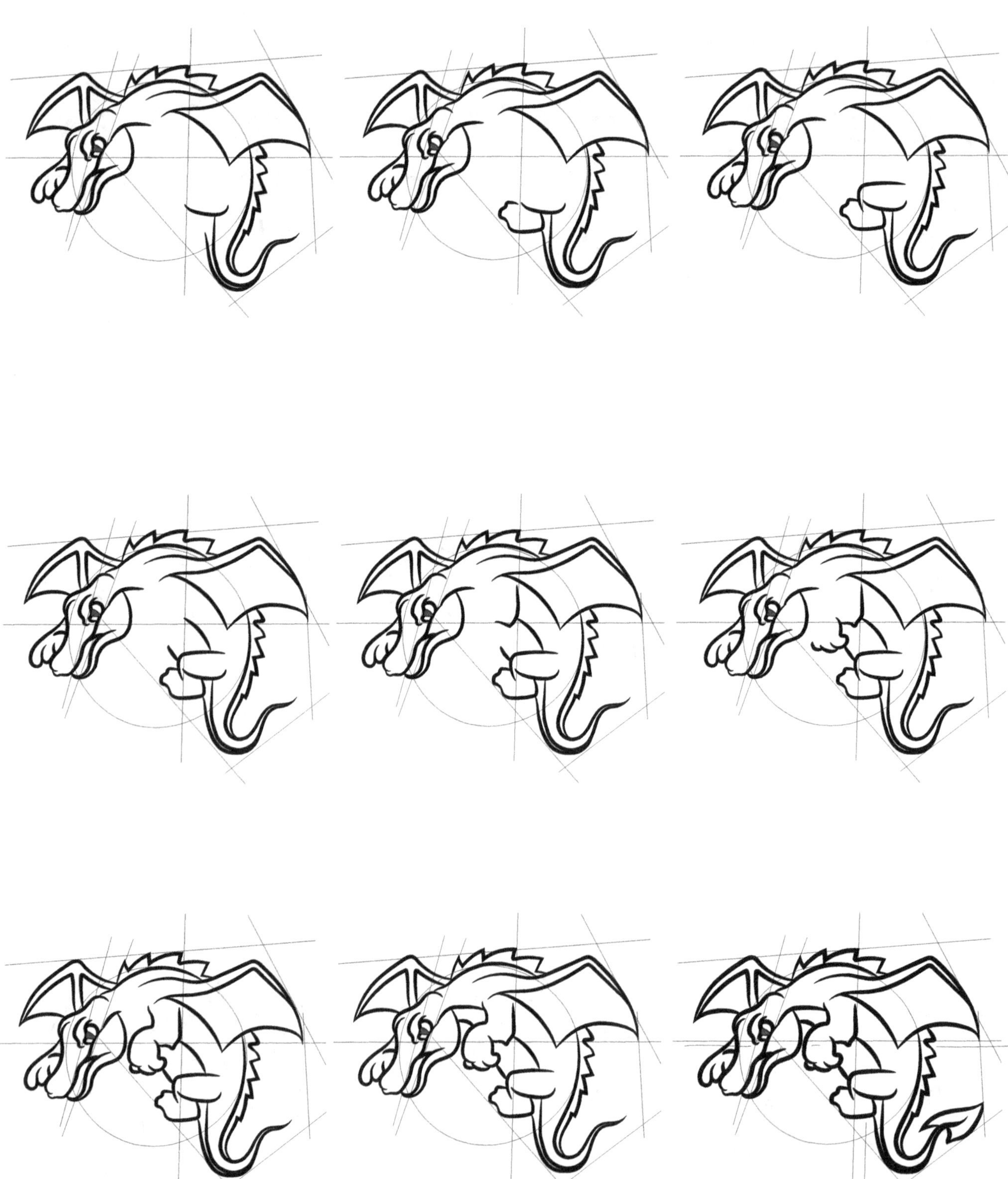

Dragons are often seen as wise and benevolent creatures, possessing ancient knowledge and offering guidance to those deemed worthy.

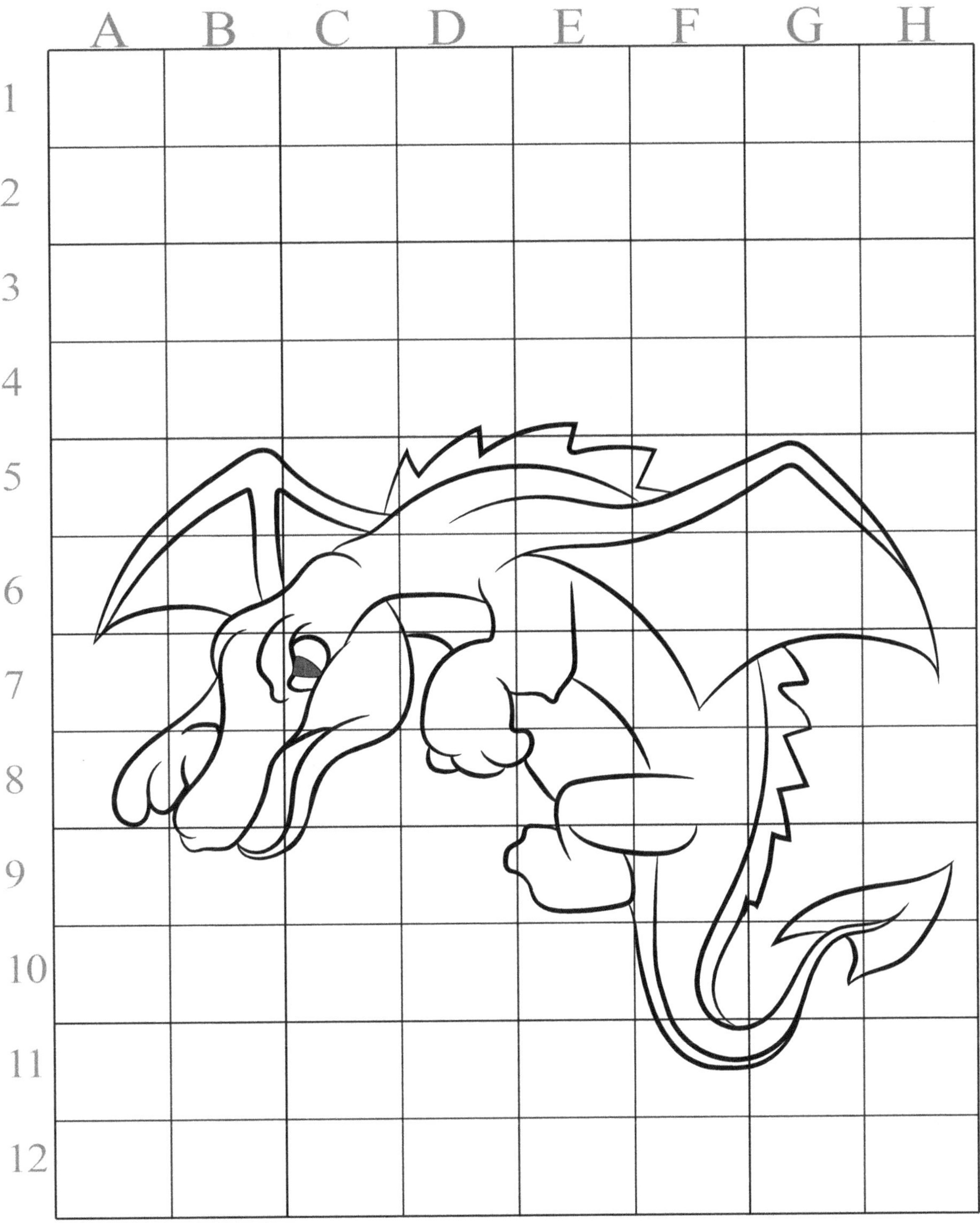

27. Try enlarging different parts of your character's body to create different effects.

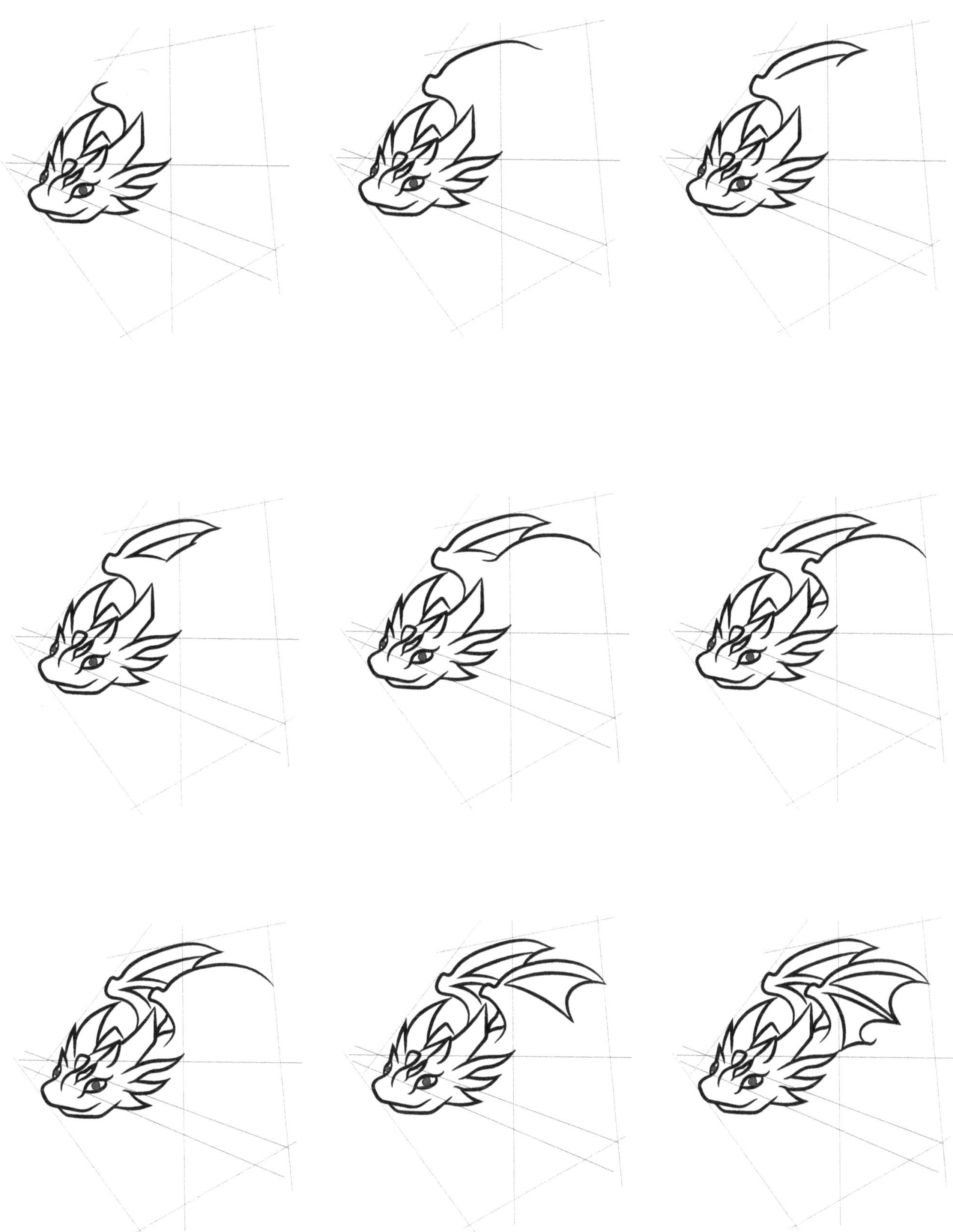

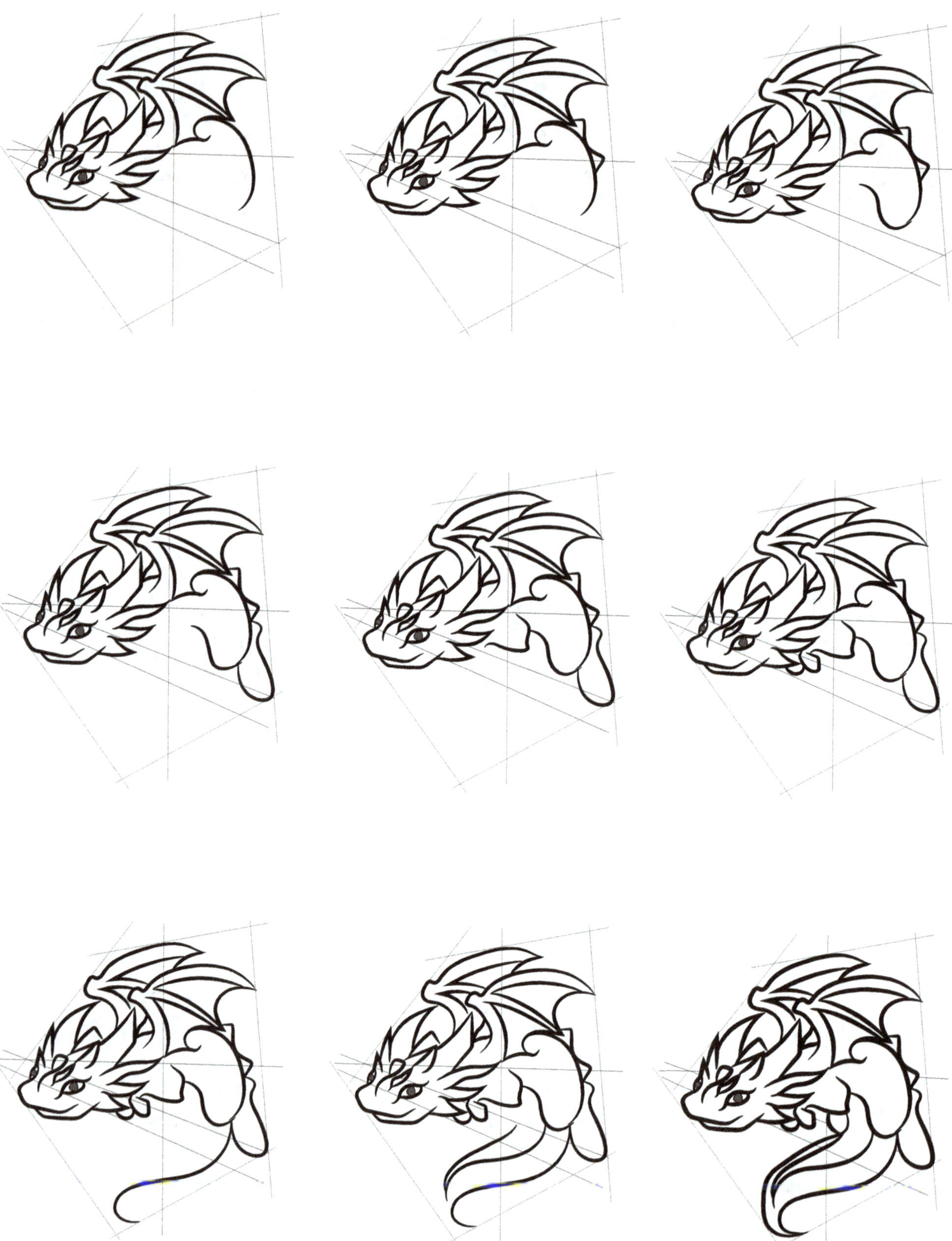

The large head of this dragon symbolizes her immense physical power and dominance over other creatures. Her formidable jaws and teeth suggest a powerful bite force, making her a fearsome predator.

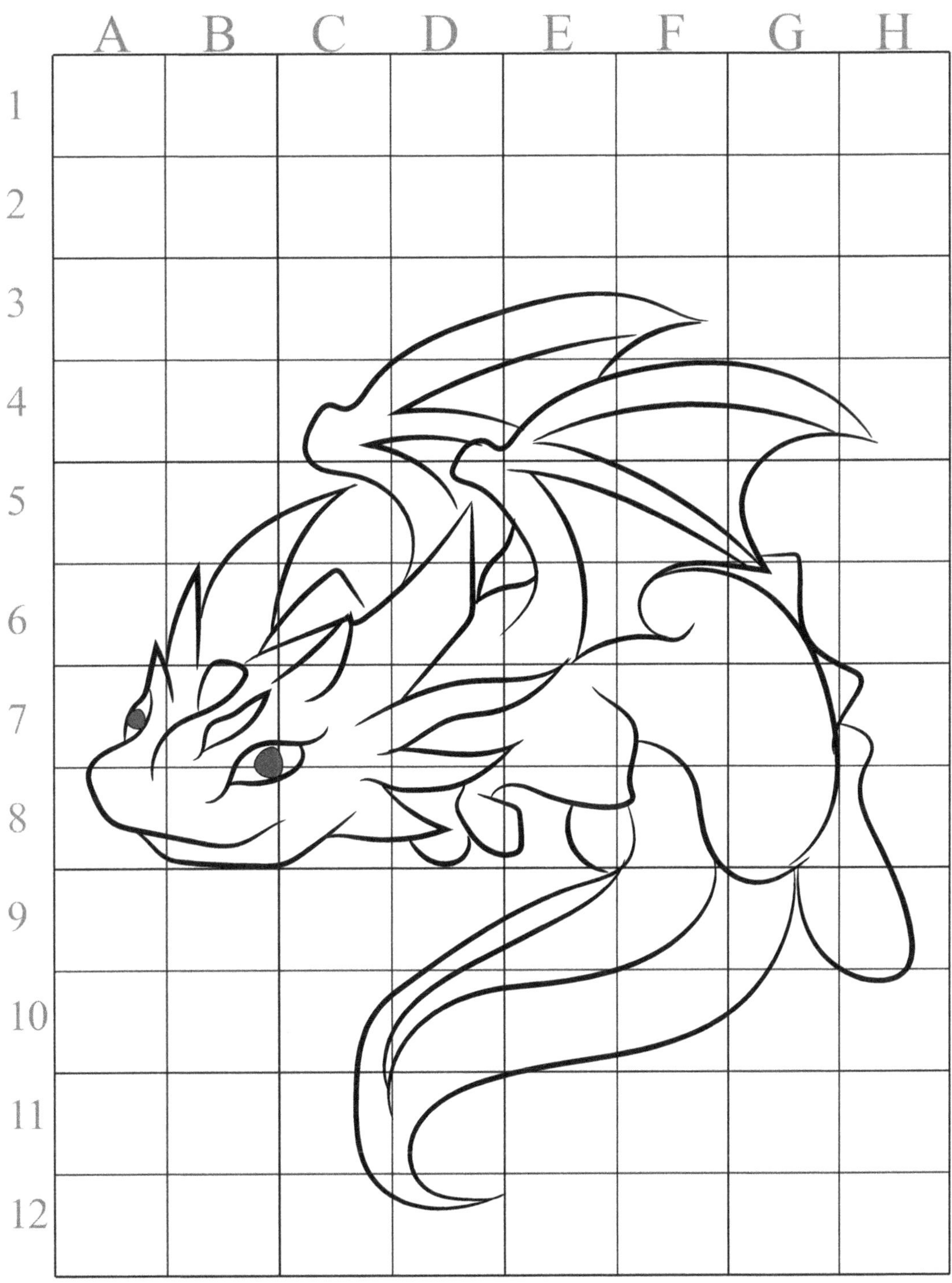

28. Separate your grid into sections to help you decide how you want to proportion your drawing.

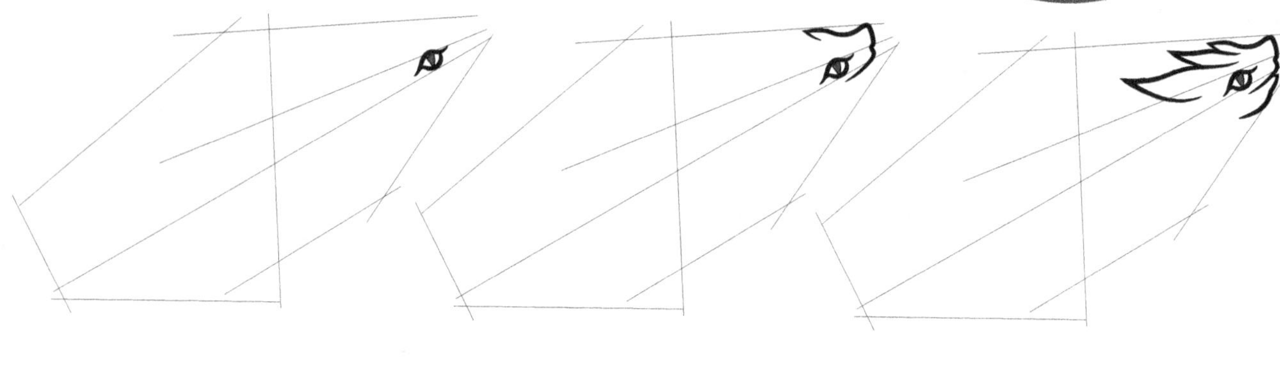

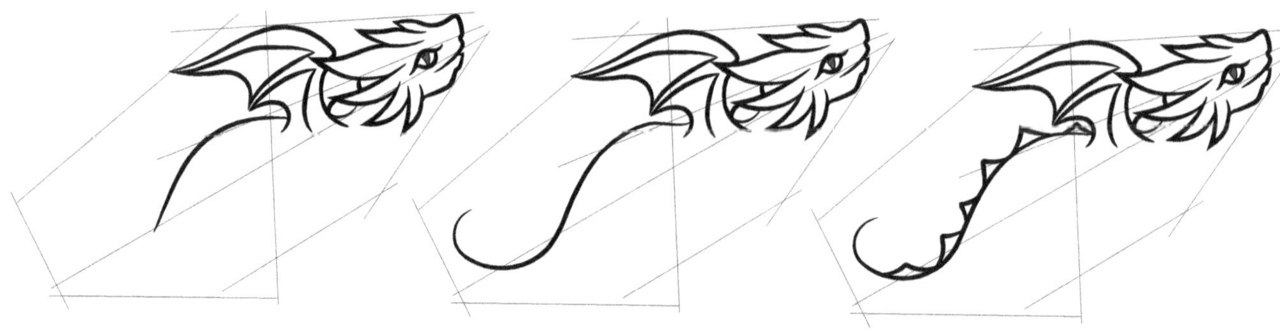

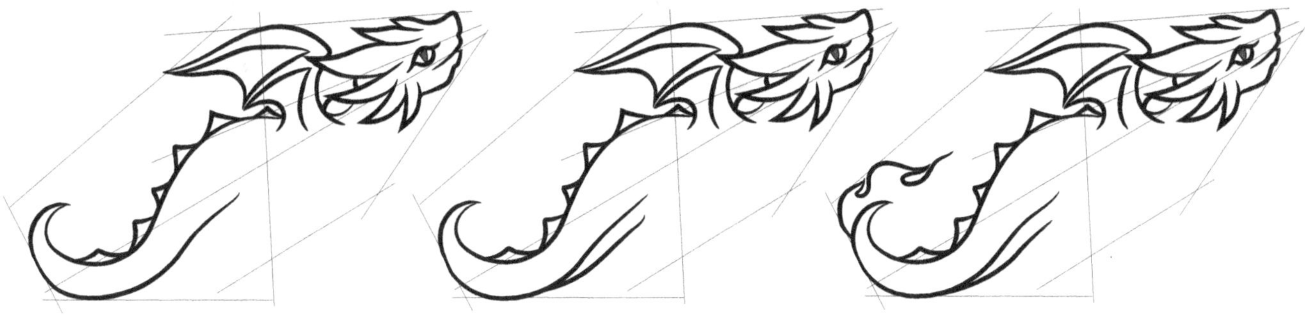

29. Creating a caricature involves exaggerating the features of your character.

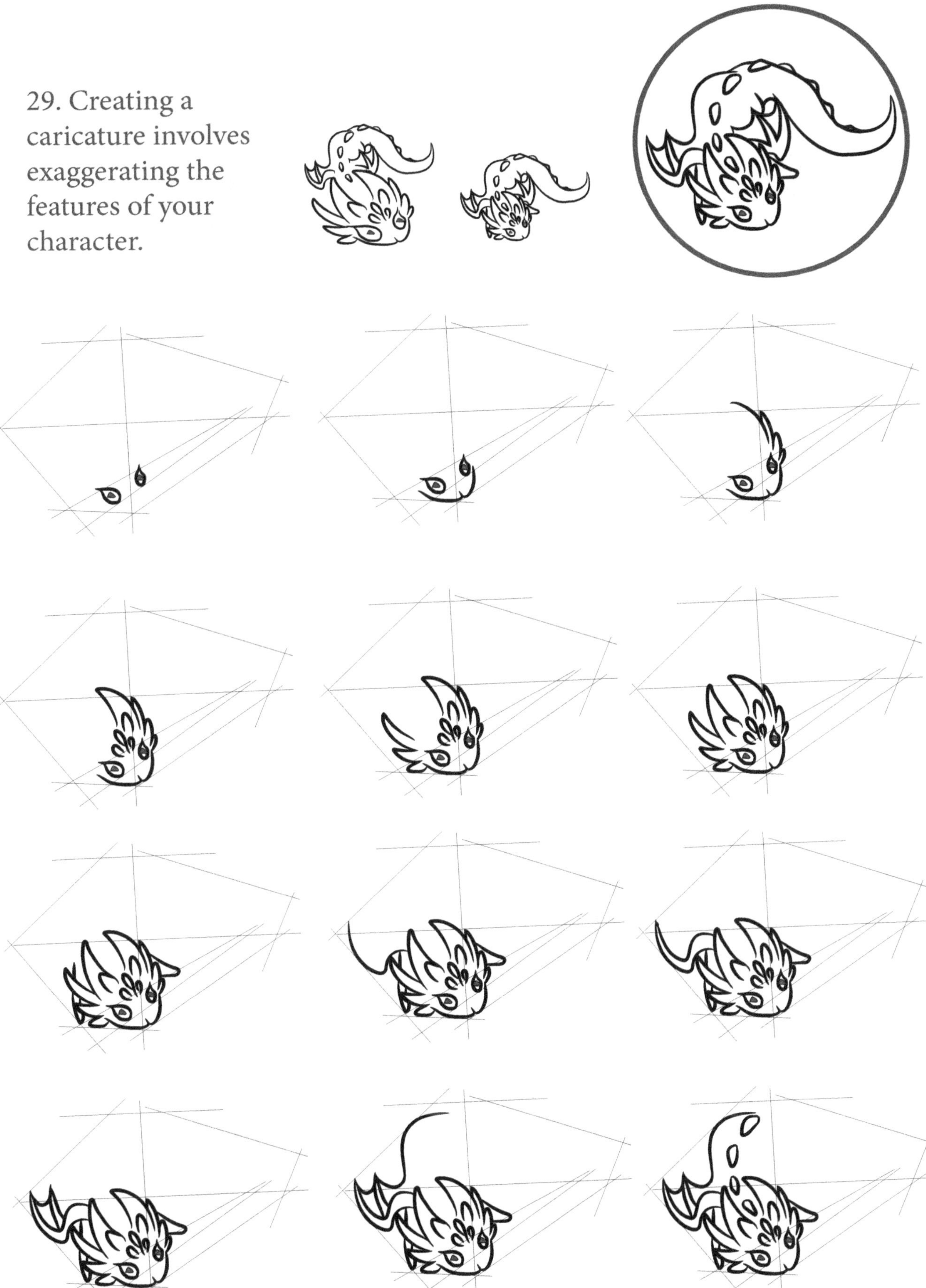

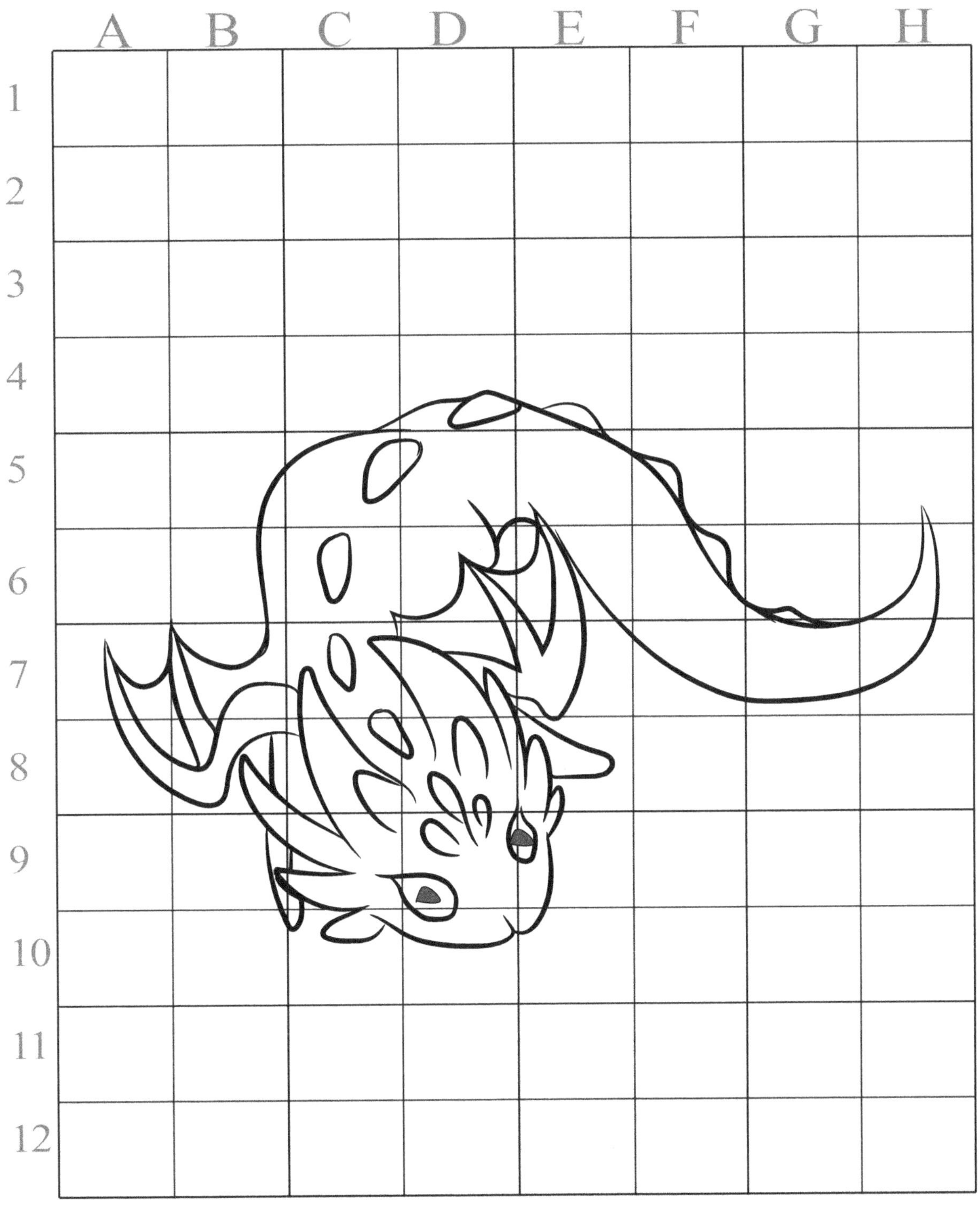

30. Give your character a curved look with
the use of an ellipse.

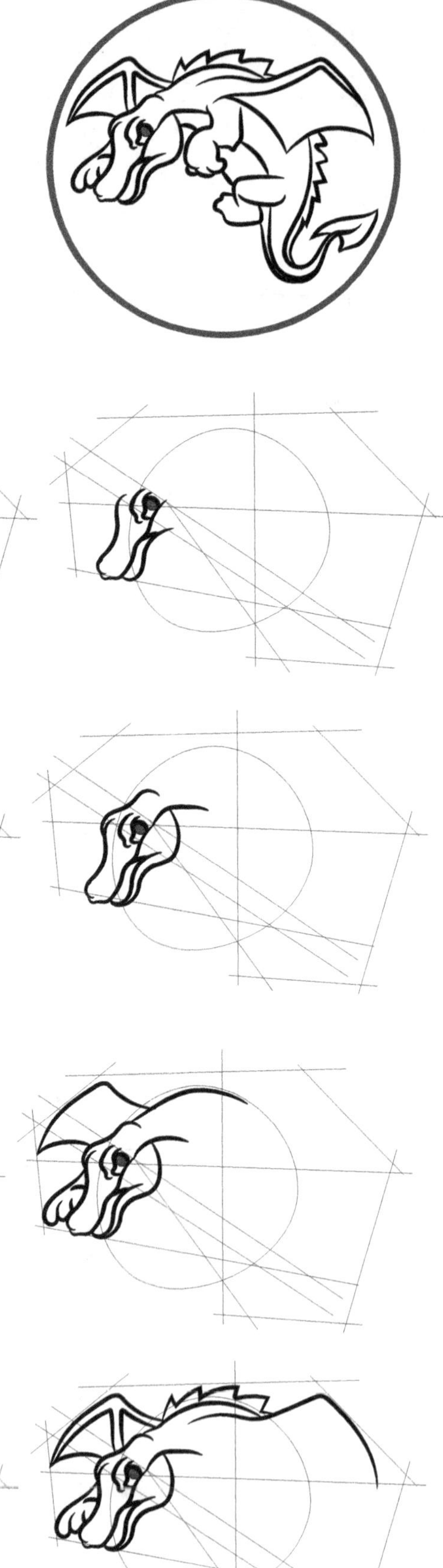

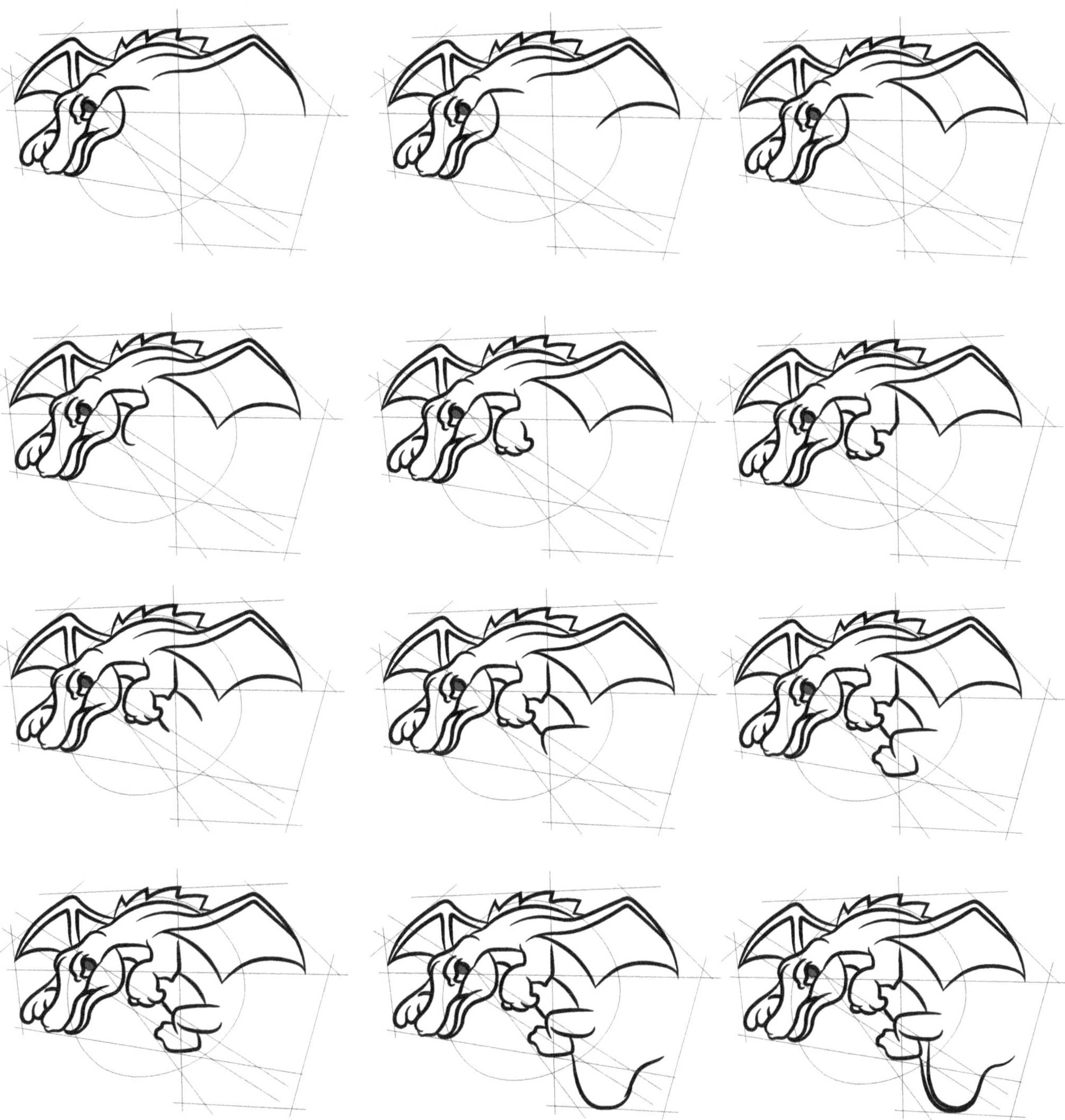

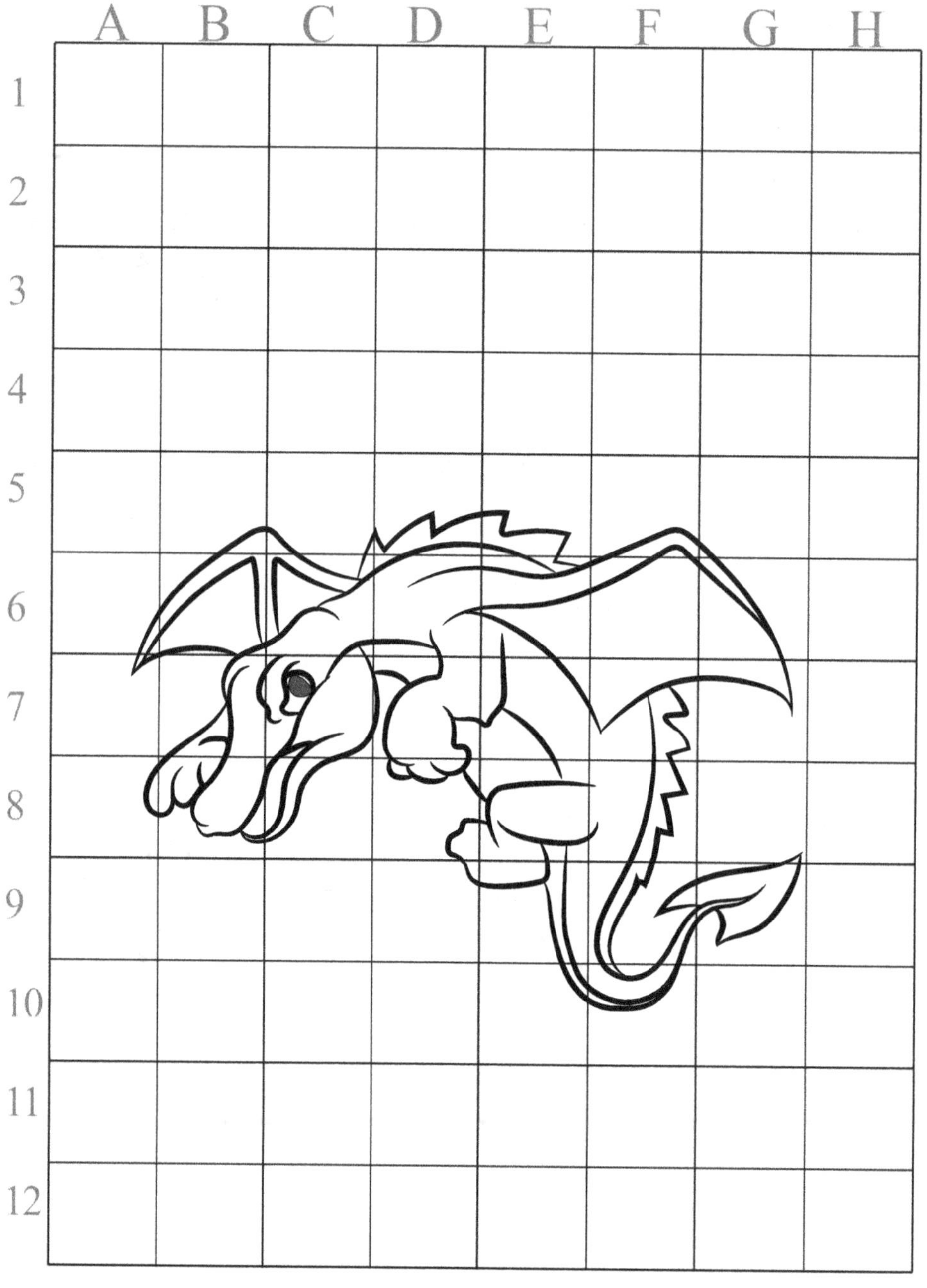

A B C D E F G H
1
2
3
4
5
6
7
8
9
10
11
12

31. Use grid lines to
show your character's
line of sight.

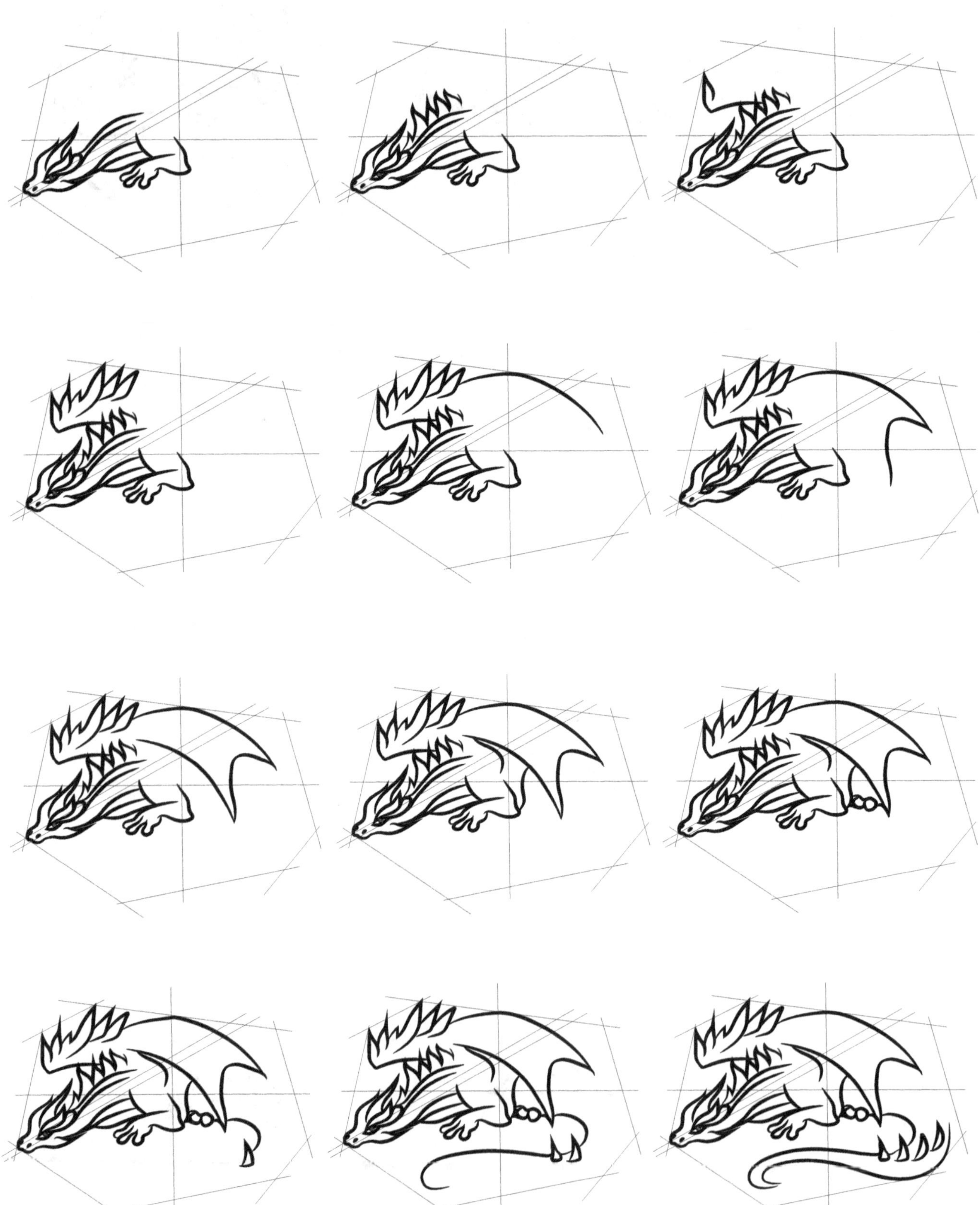

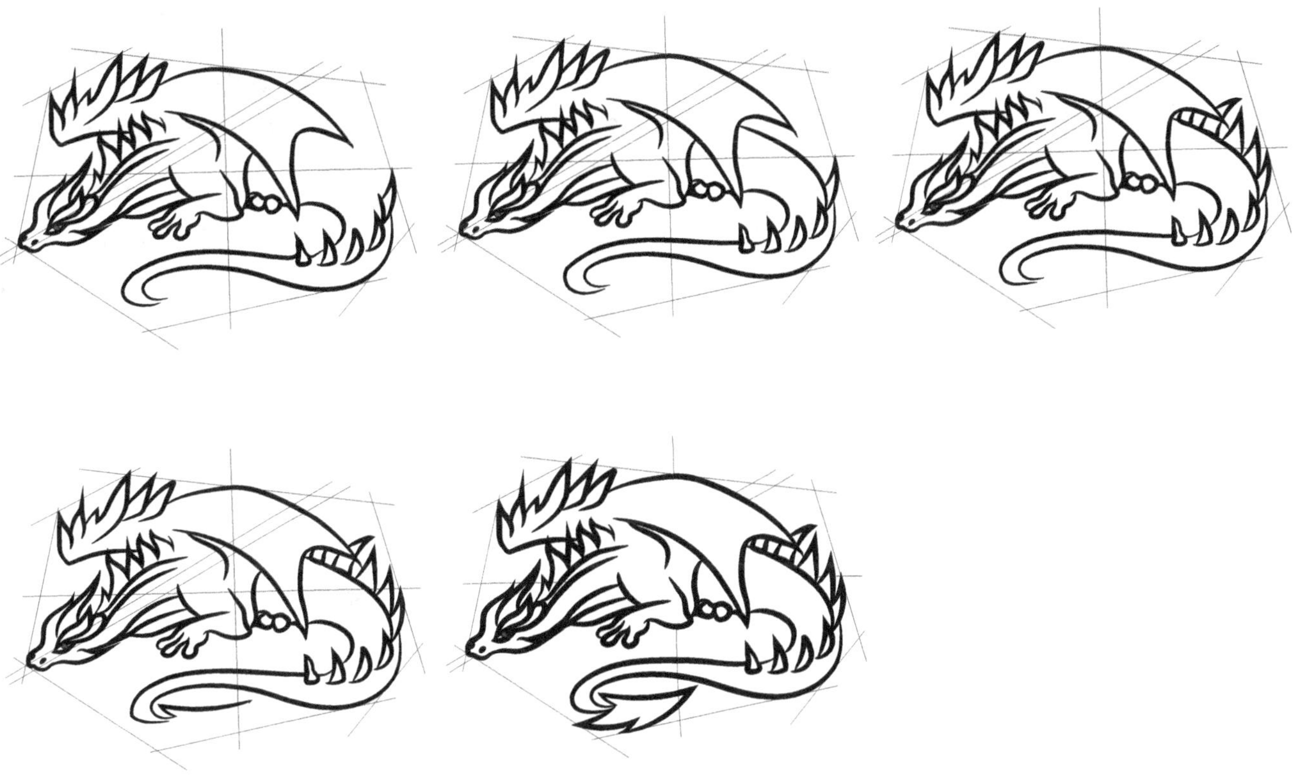

32. Adding a flame
coming out of your
dragon's mouth can
produce a very nice effect.

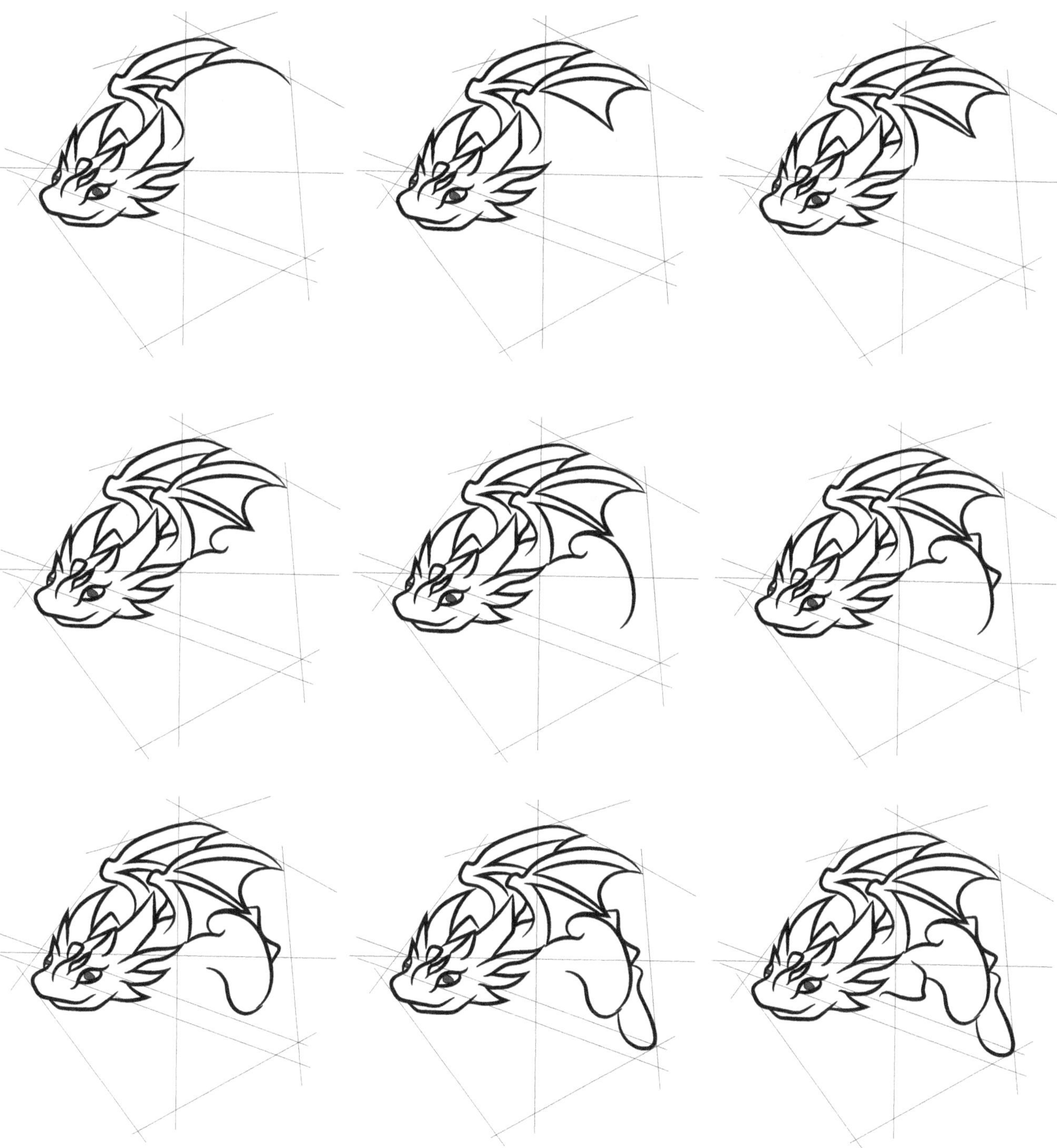

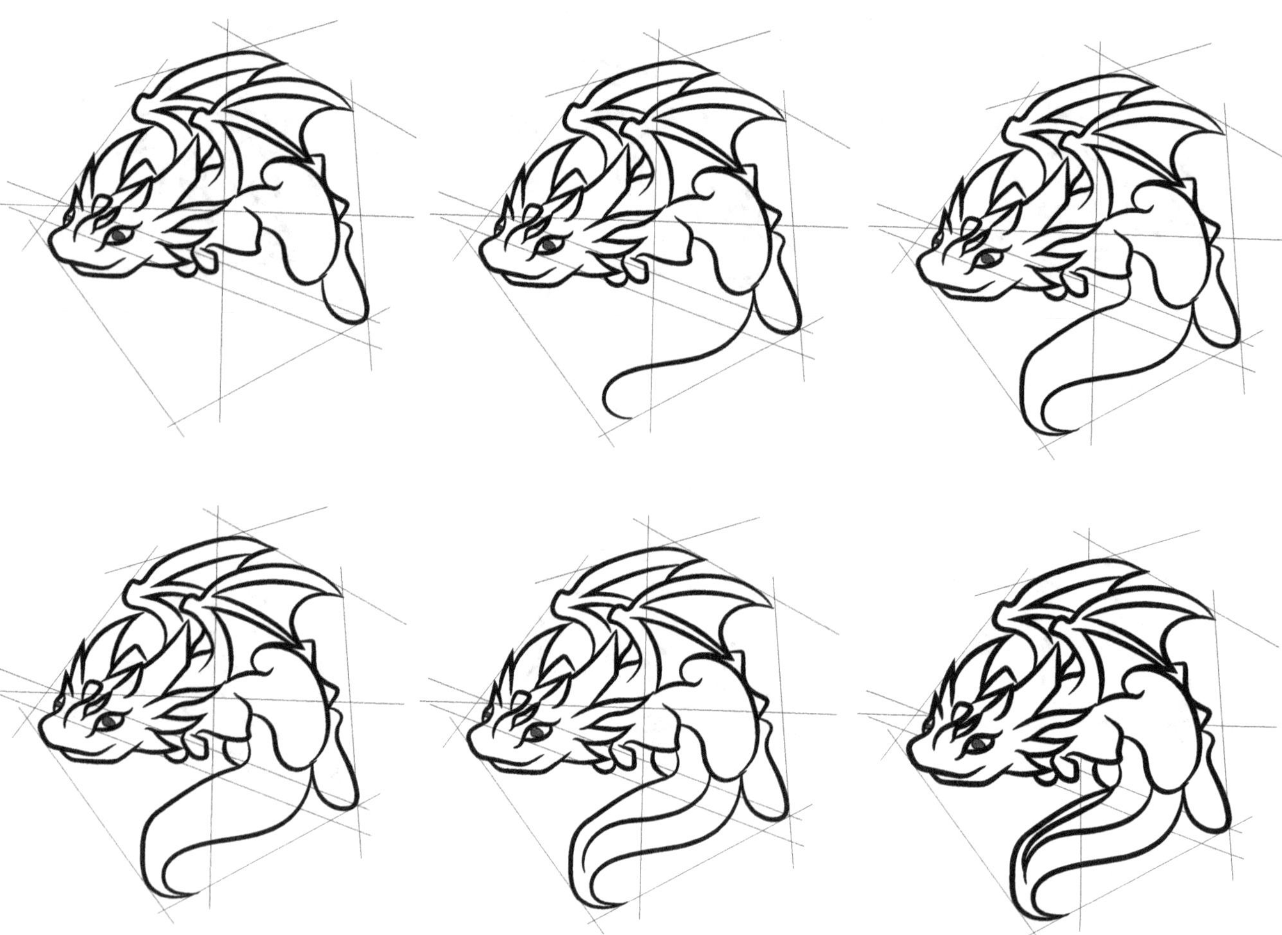

A large head can also signify heightened intelligence and wisdom. In many stories, dragons with large heads are depicted as wise beings with vast knowledge and magical abilities.

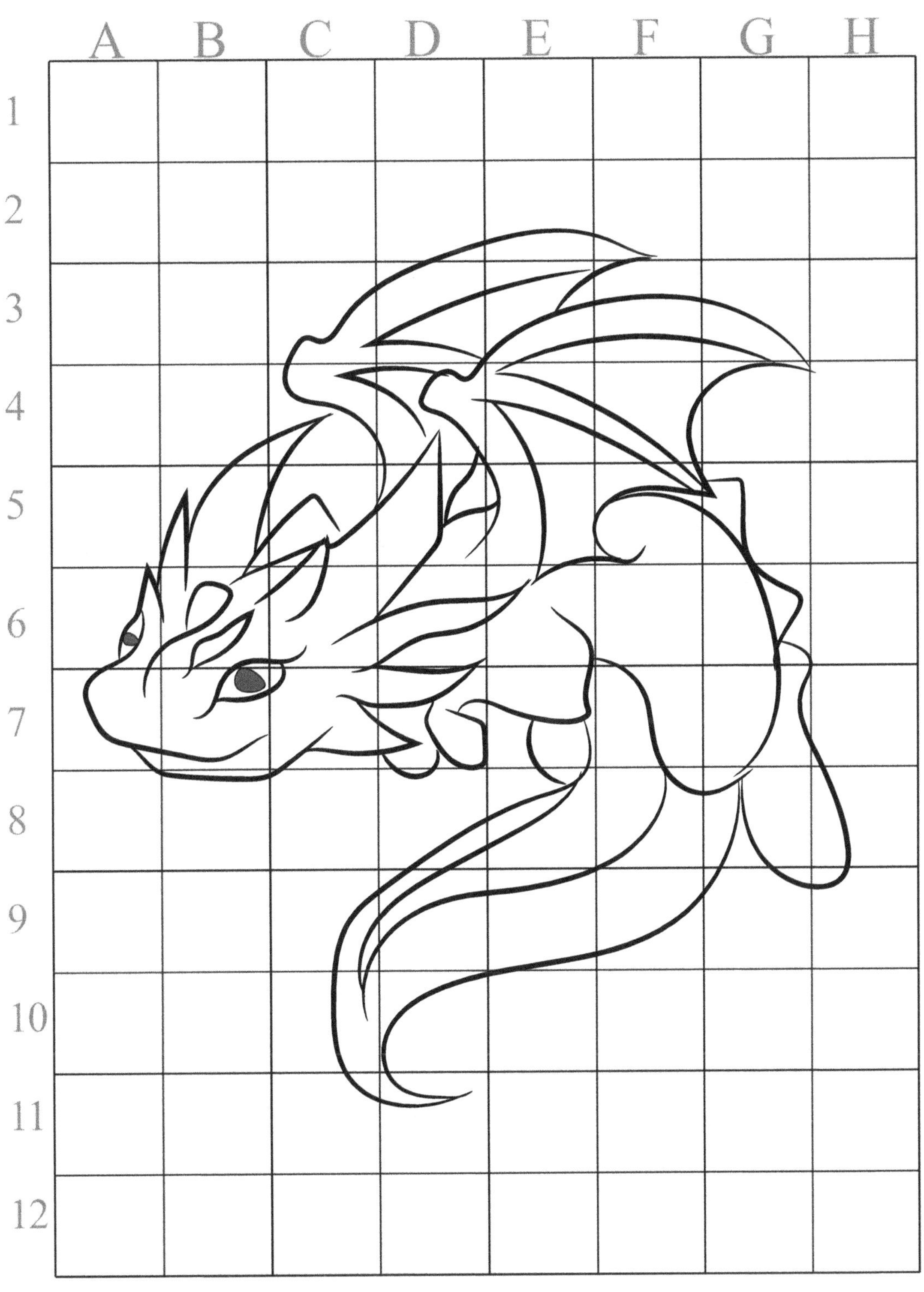

33. Add extra features to your character to make it look more original.

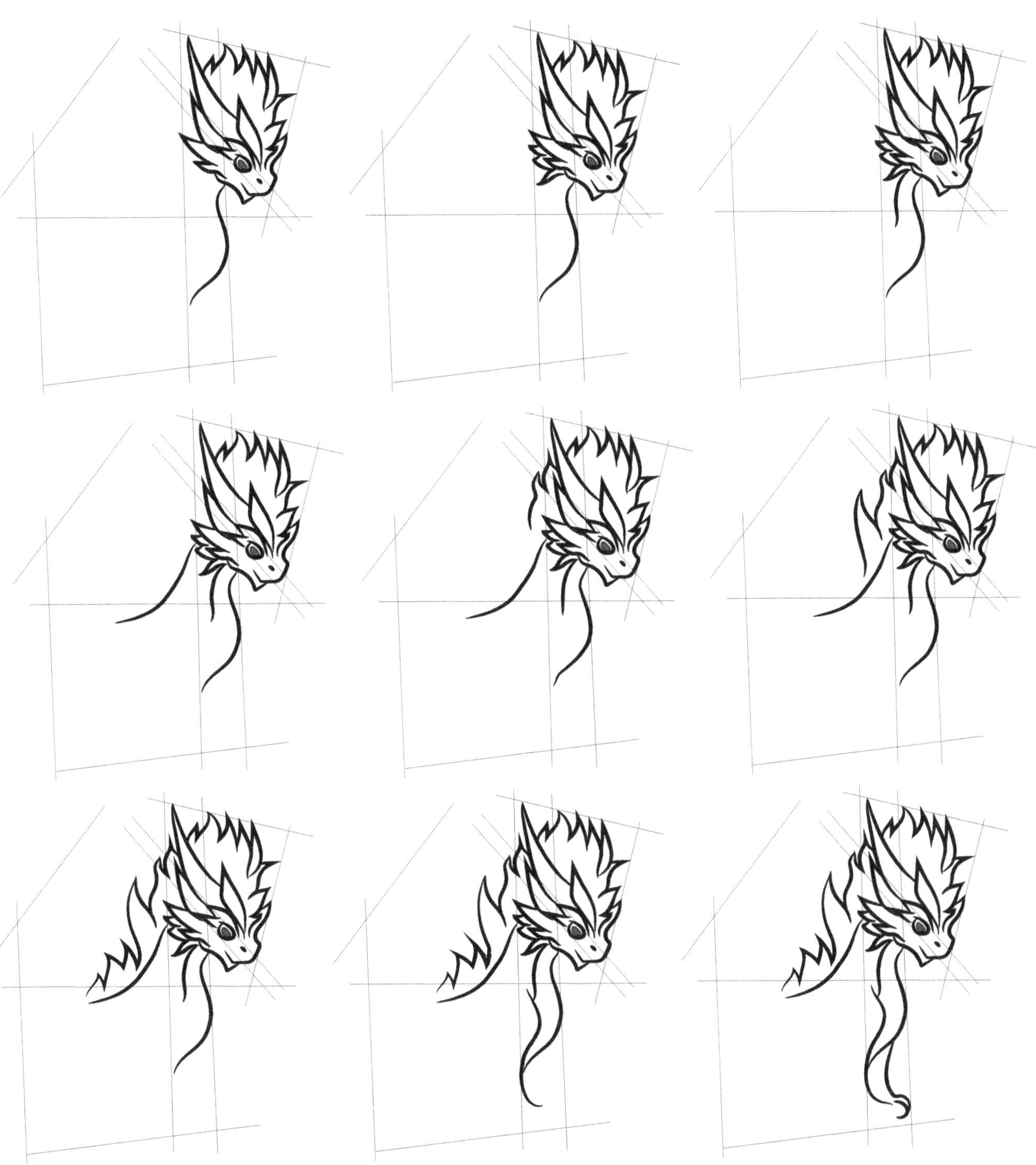

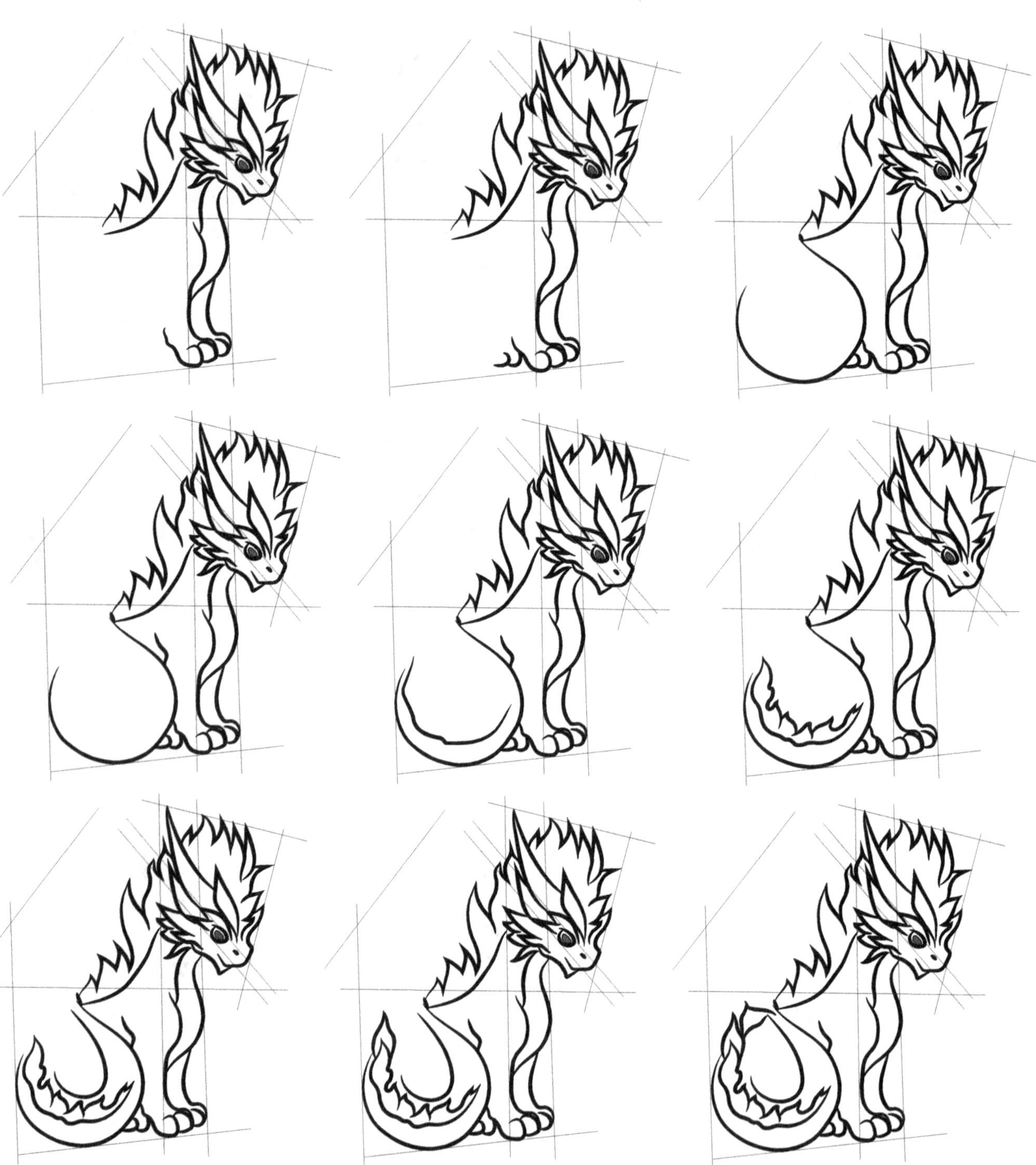

34. Try altering your character slightly to create a different look.

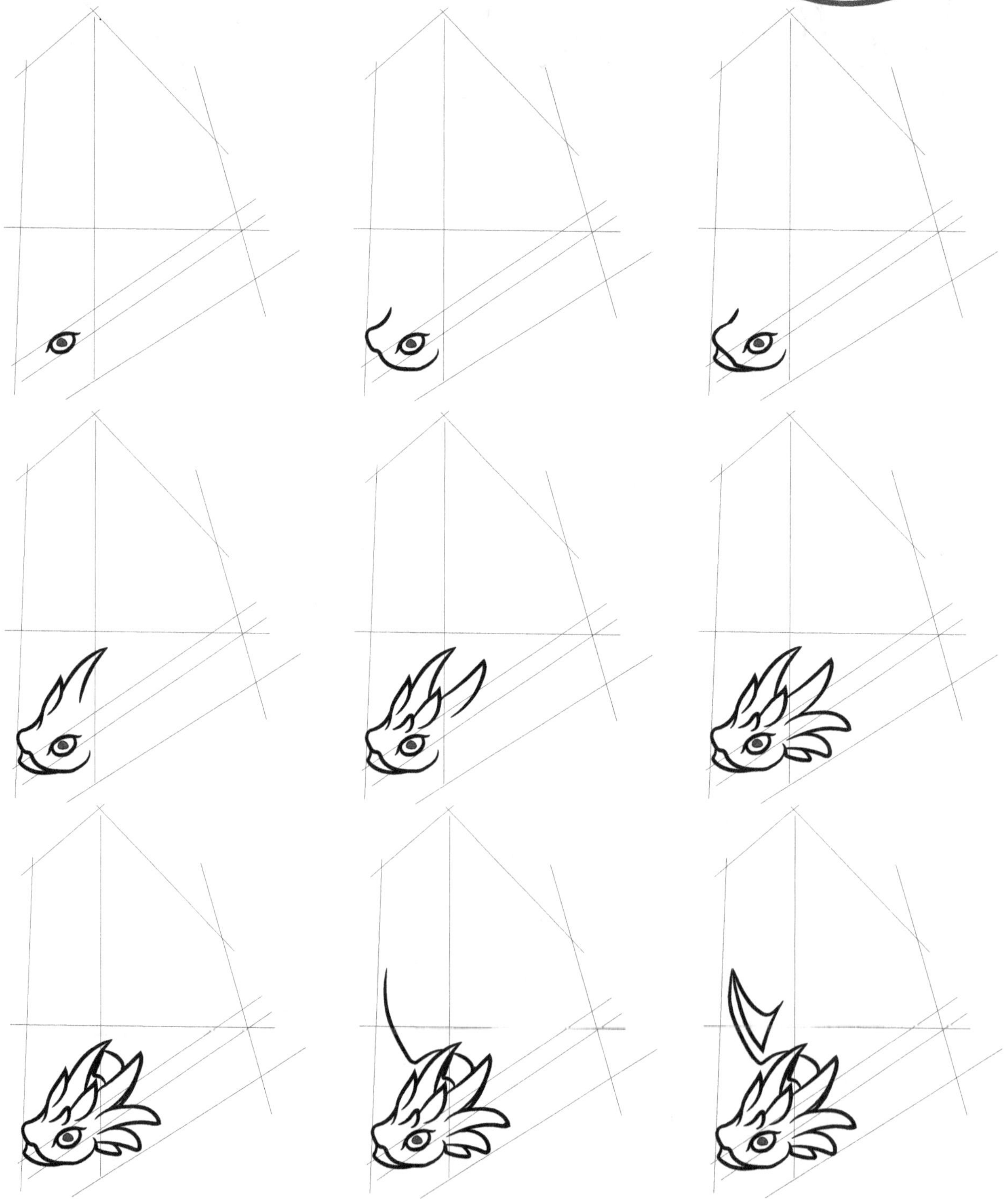

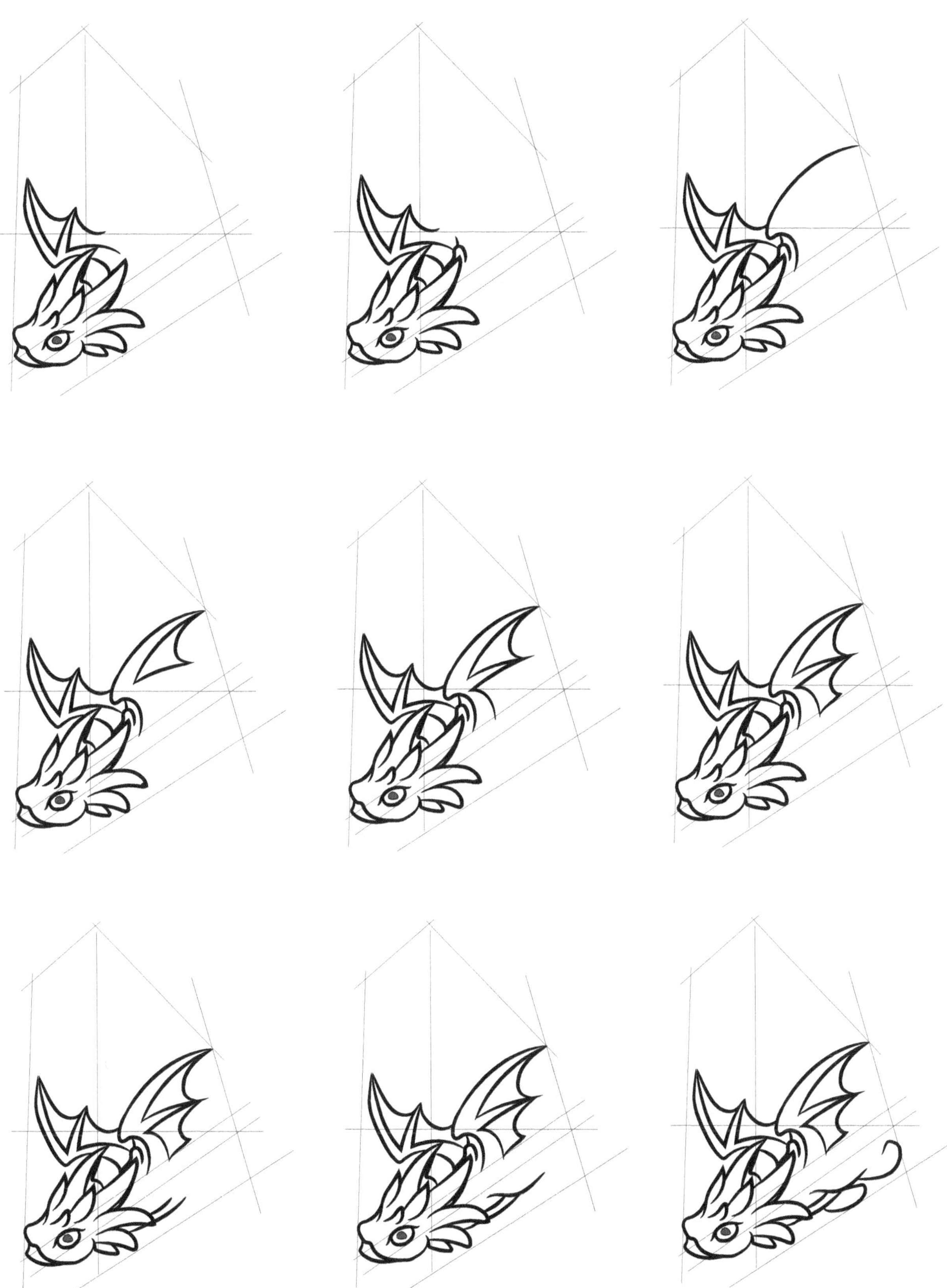

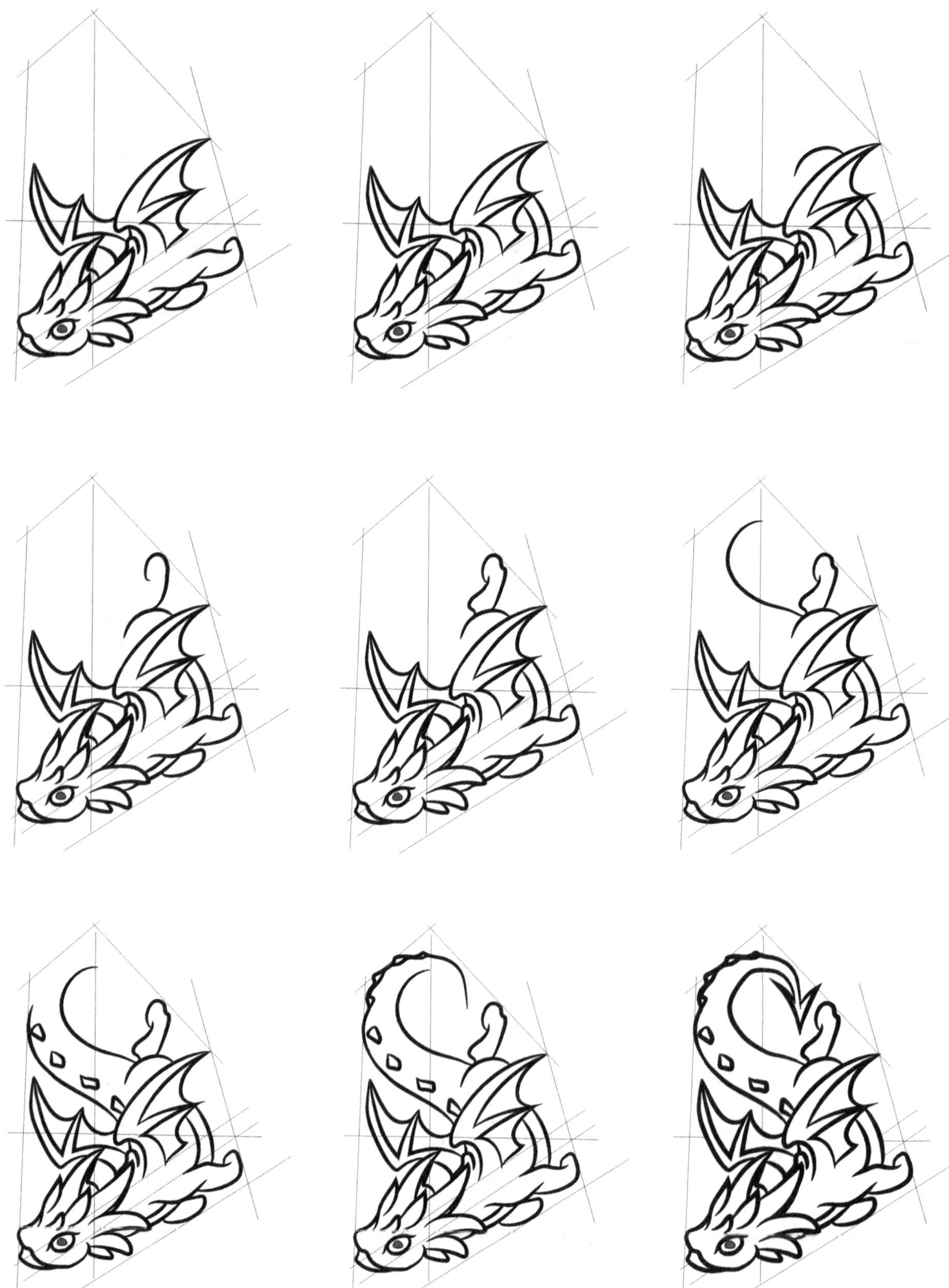

Eastern dragons are typically seen as benevolent and wise, whereas Western dragons are often depicted as malevolent and dangerous.

35. Starting your drawing with the eyes will
help your initial sketch to take shape.

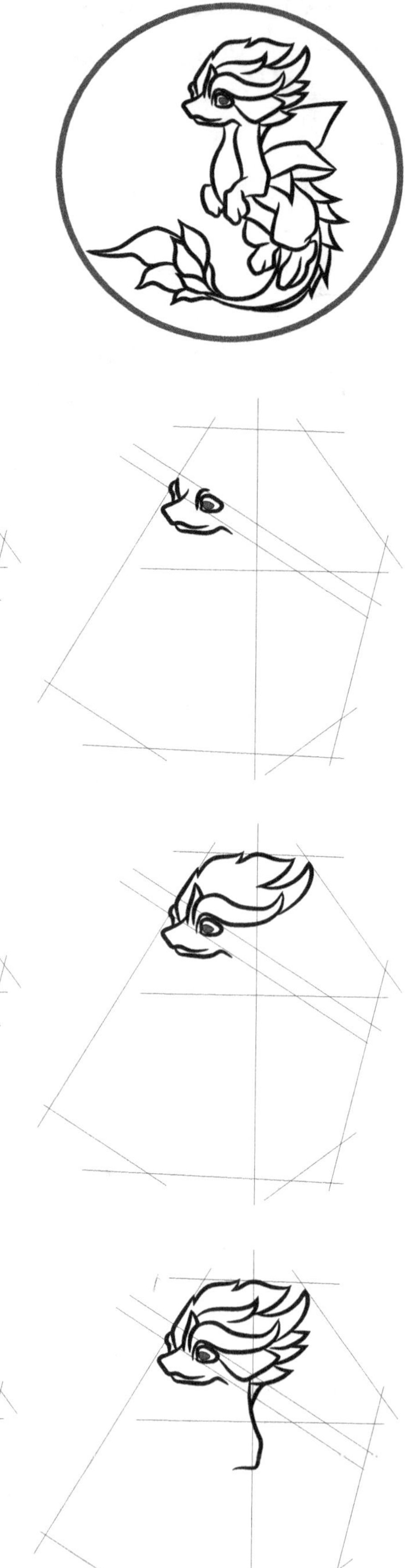

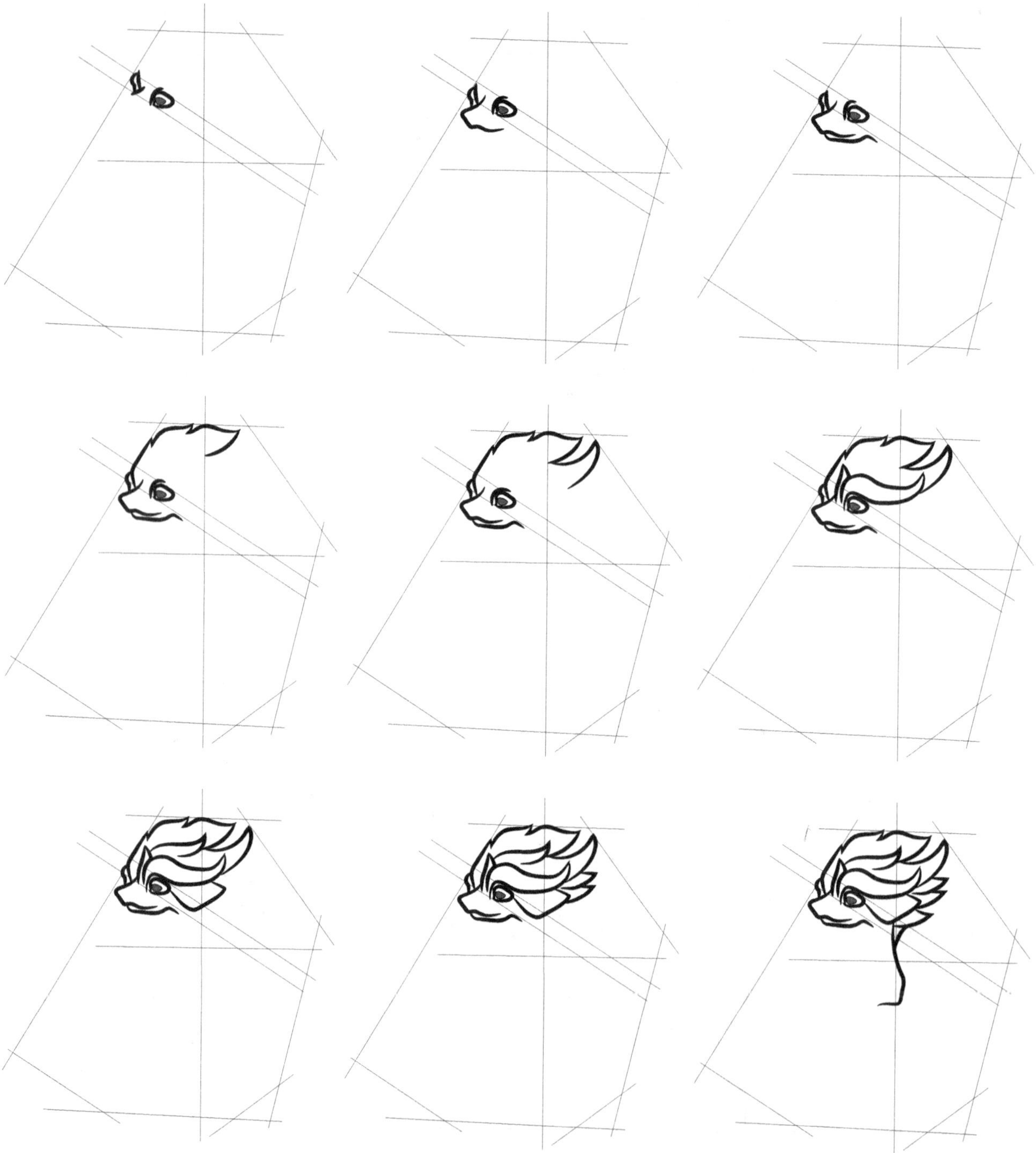

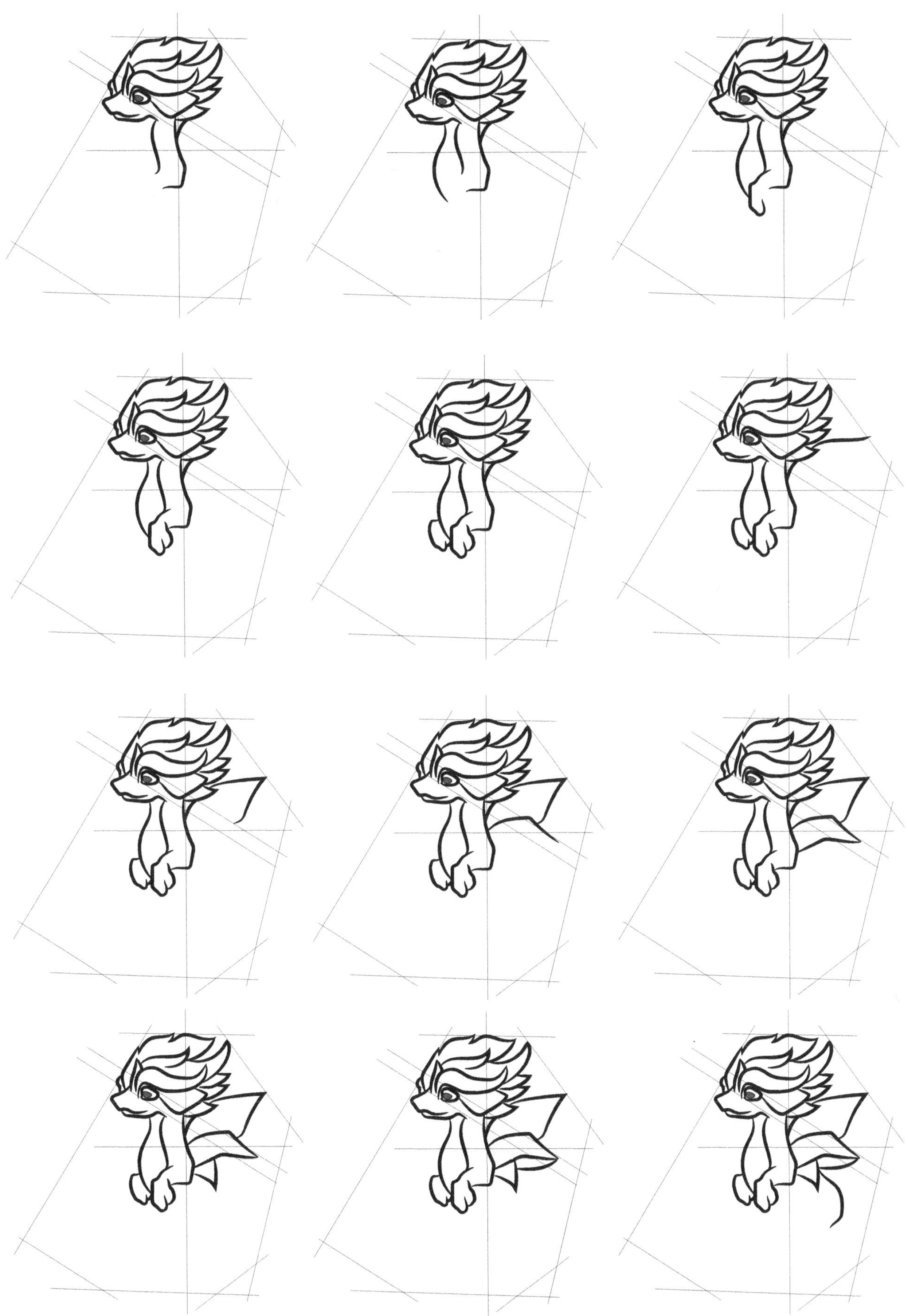

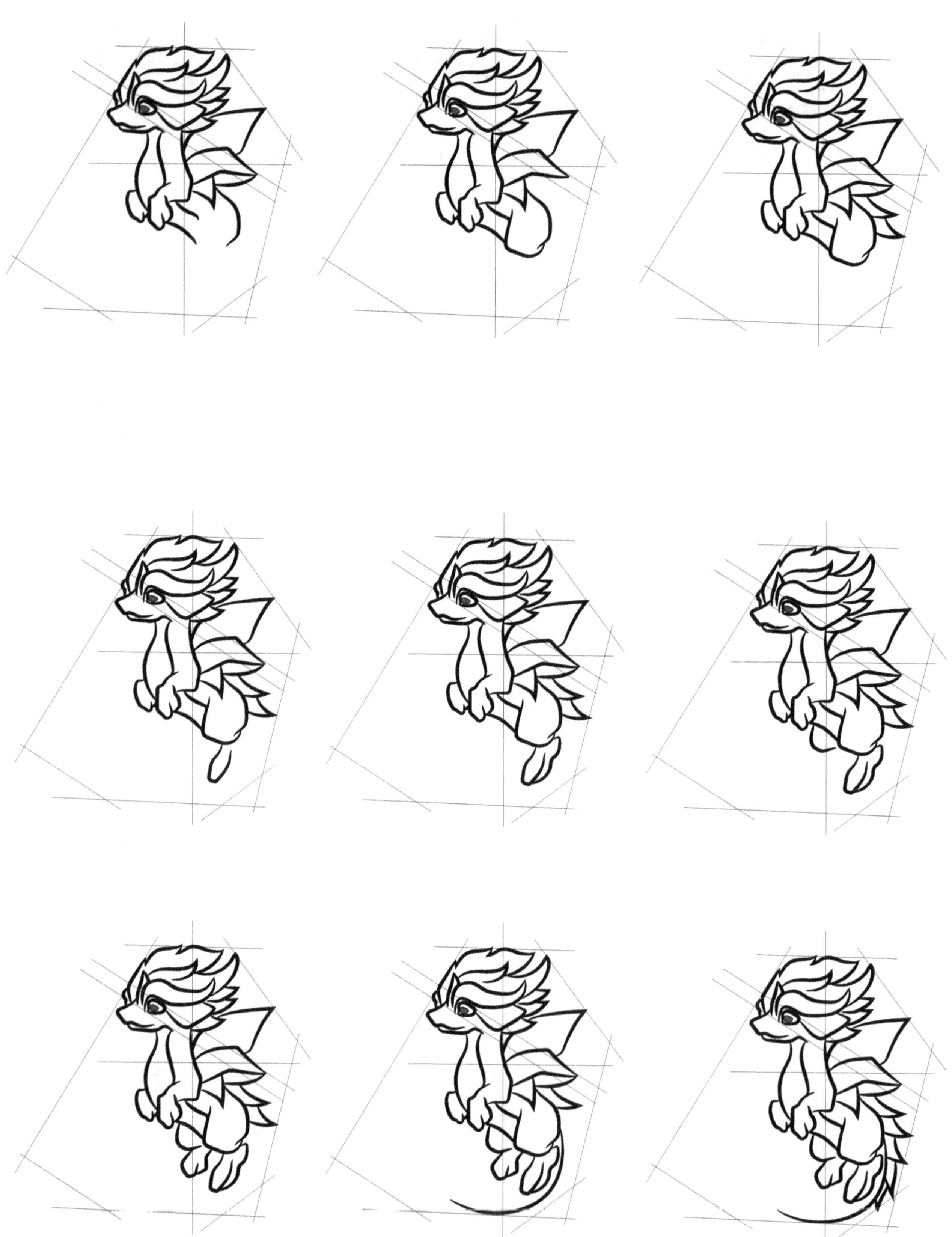

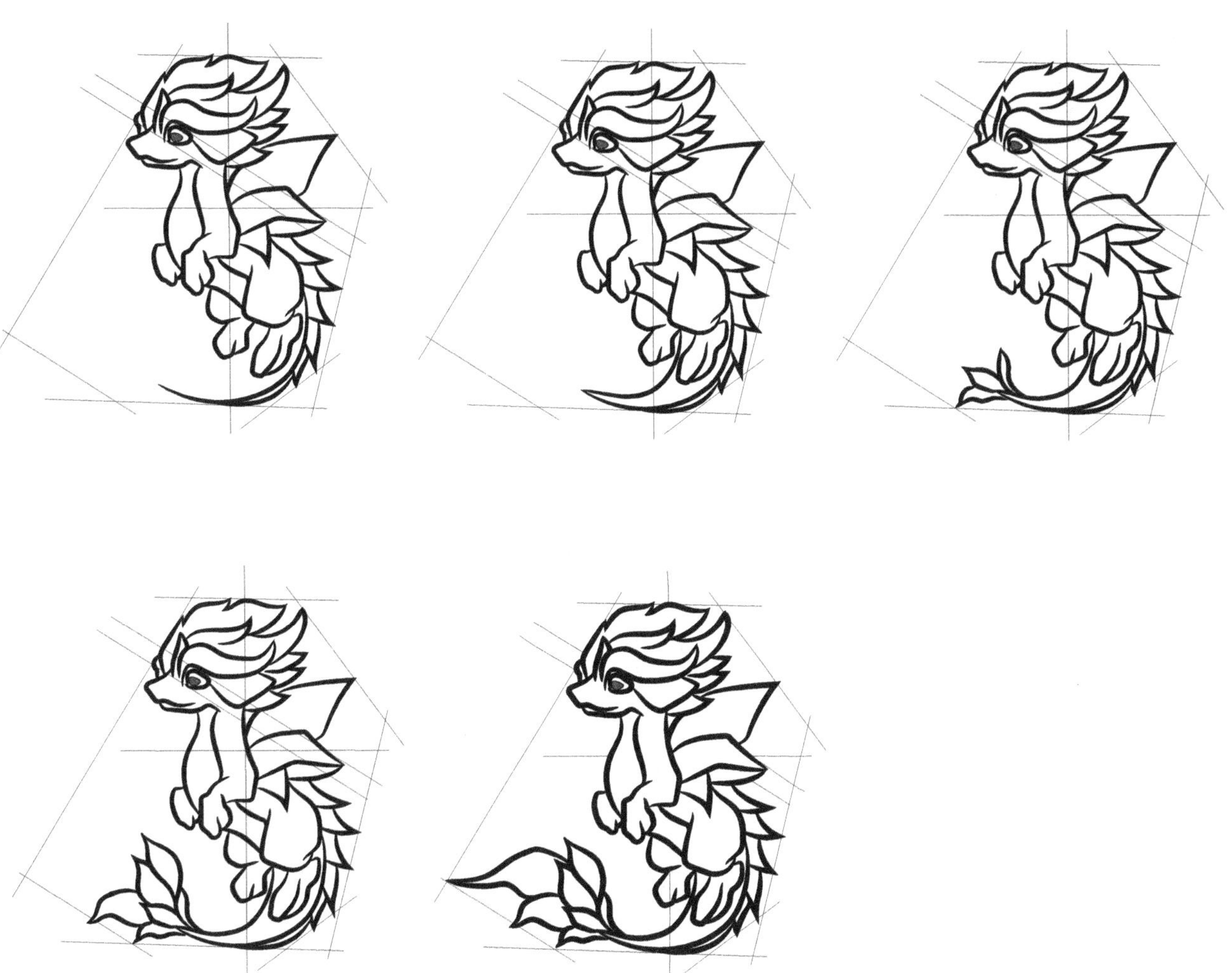

Eastern dragons are typically seen as benevolent and wise, whereas Western dragons are often depicted as malevolent and dangerous.

36. Use thinner lines to
show greater detail.

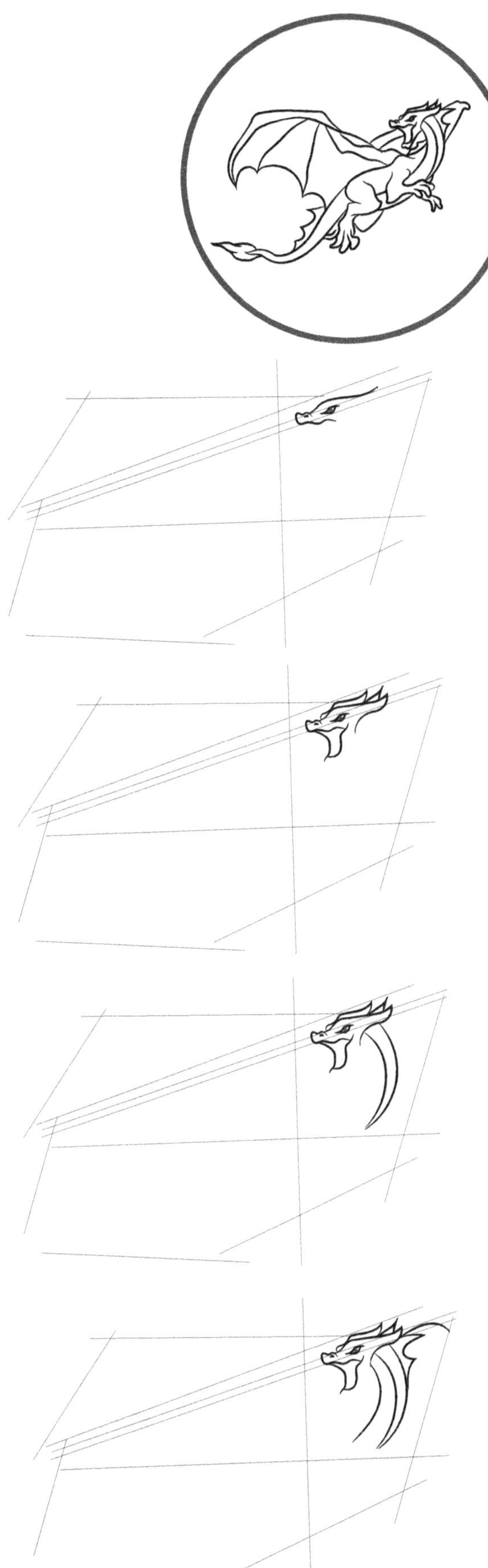

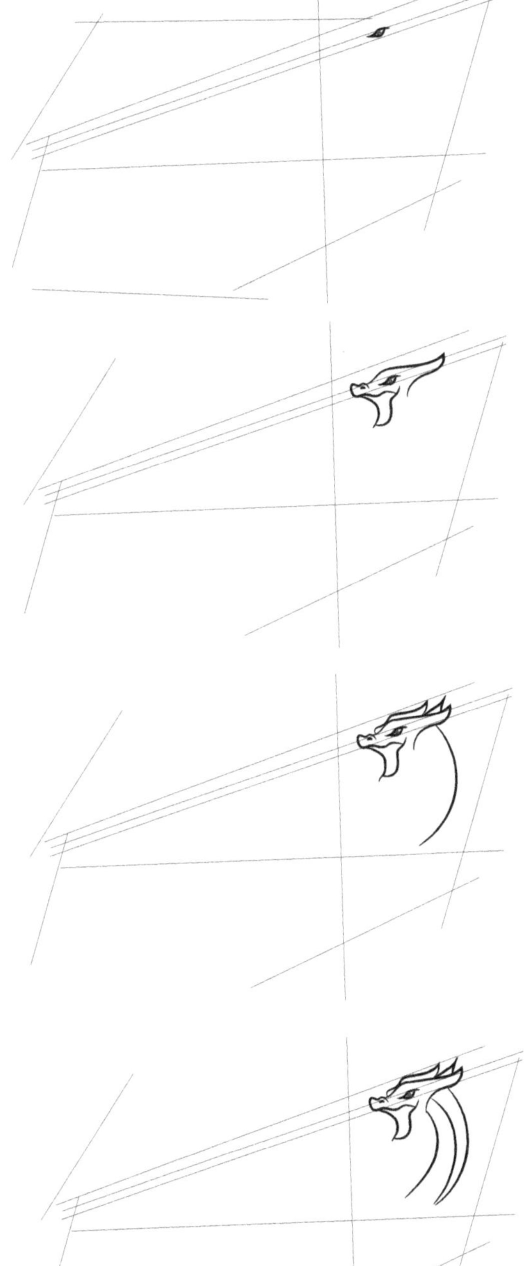

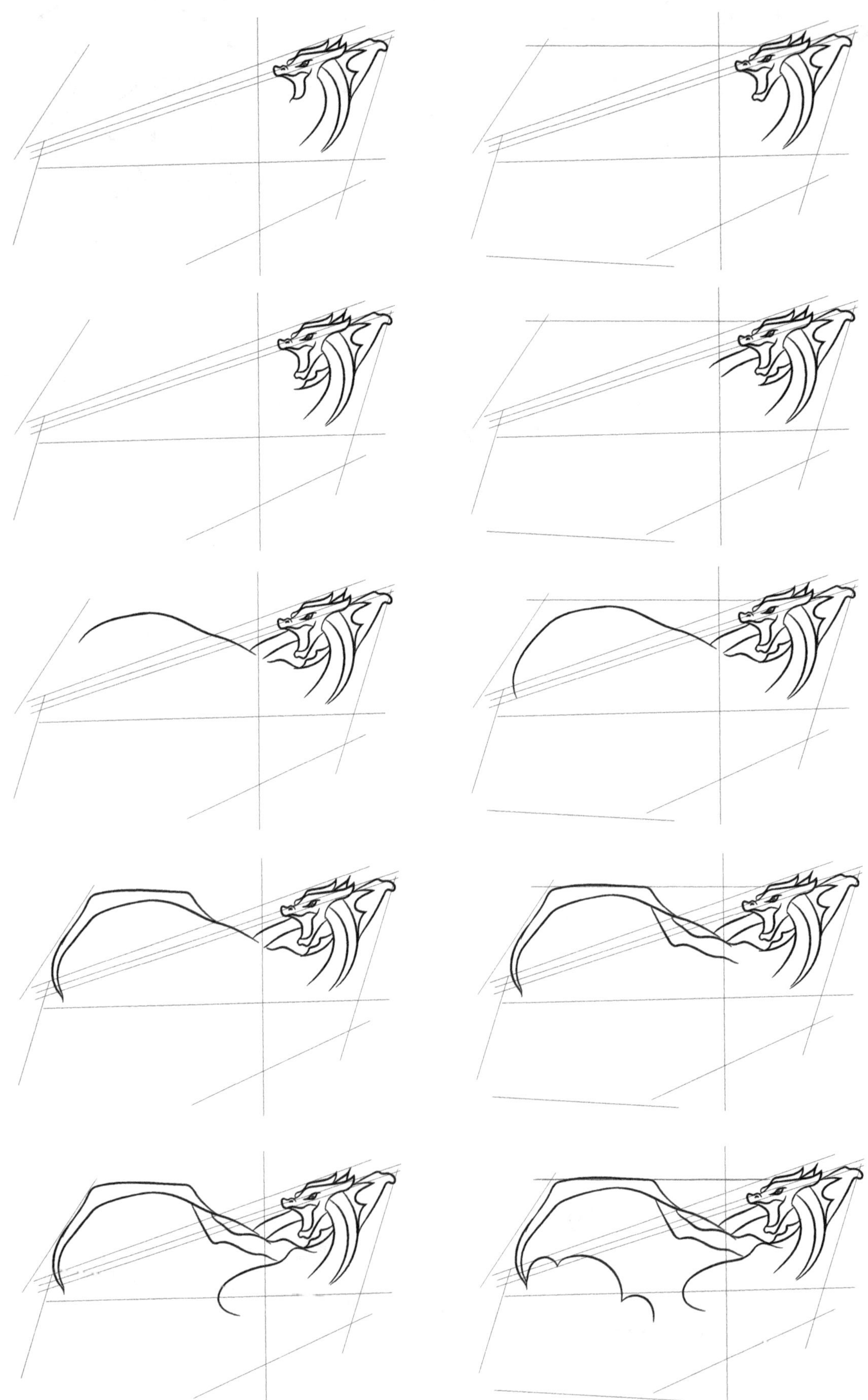

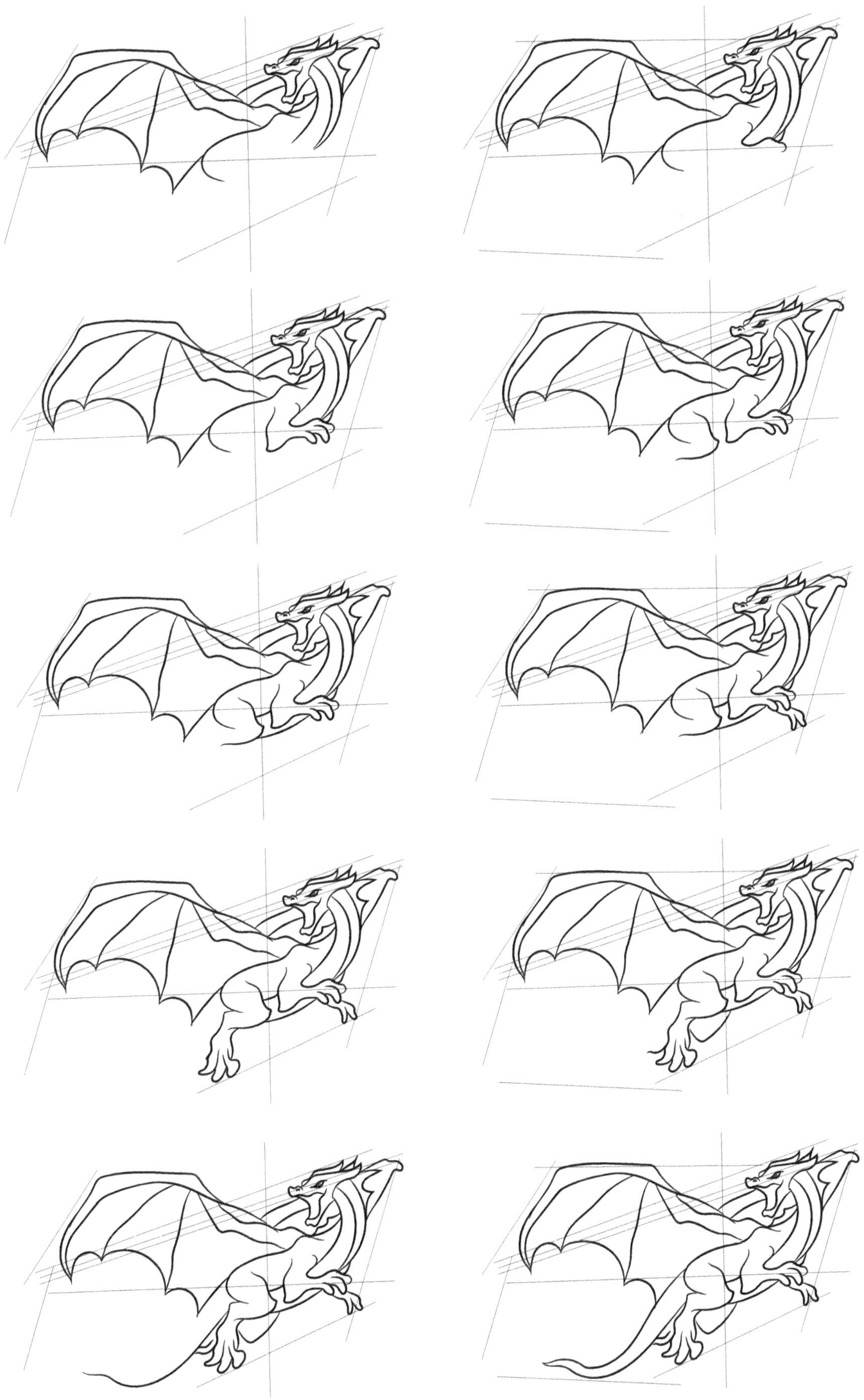

Dragons with large wings are a captivating and iconic depiction found in various mythologies and fantasy stories worldwide. These dragons are known for their impressive wingspans, allowing them to soar through the skies and dominate both land and air.

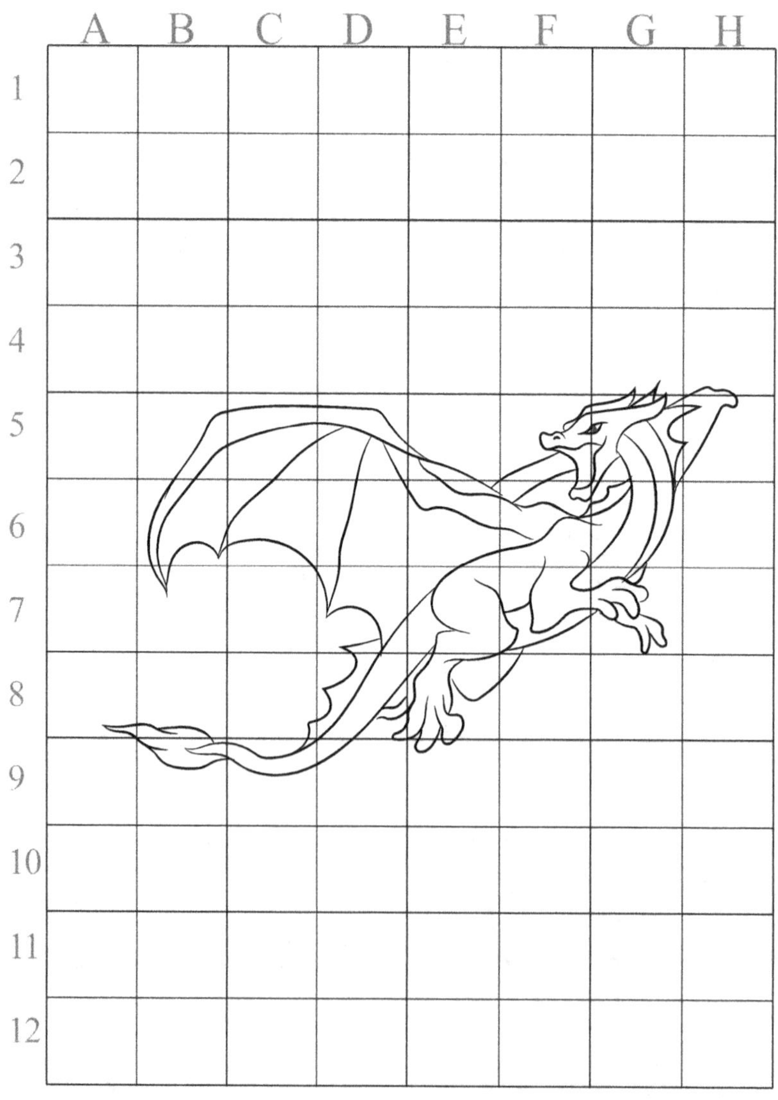

37. Choosing how you represent hands and feet on your character can have an impact on your character's body language.

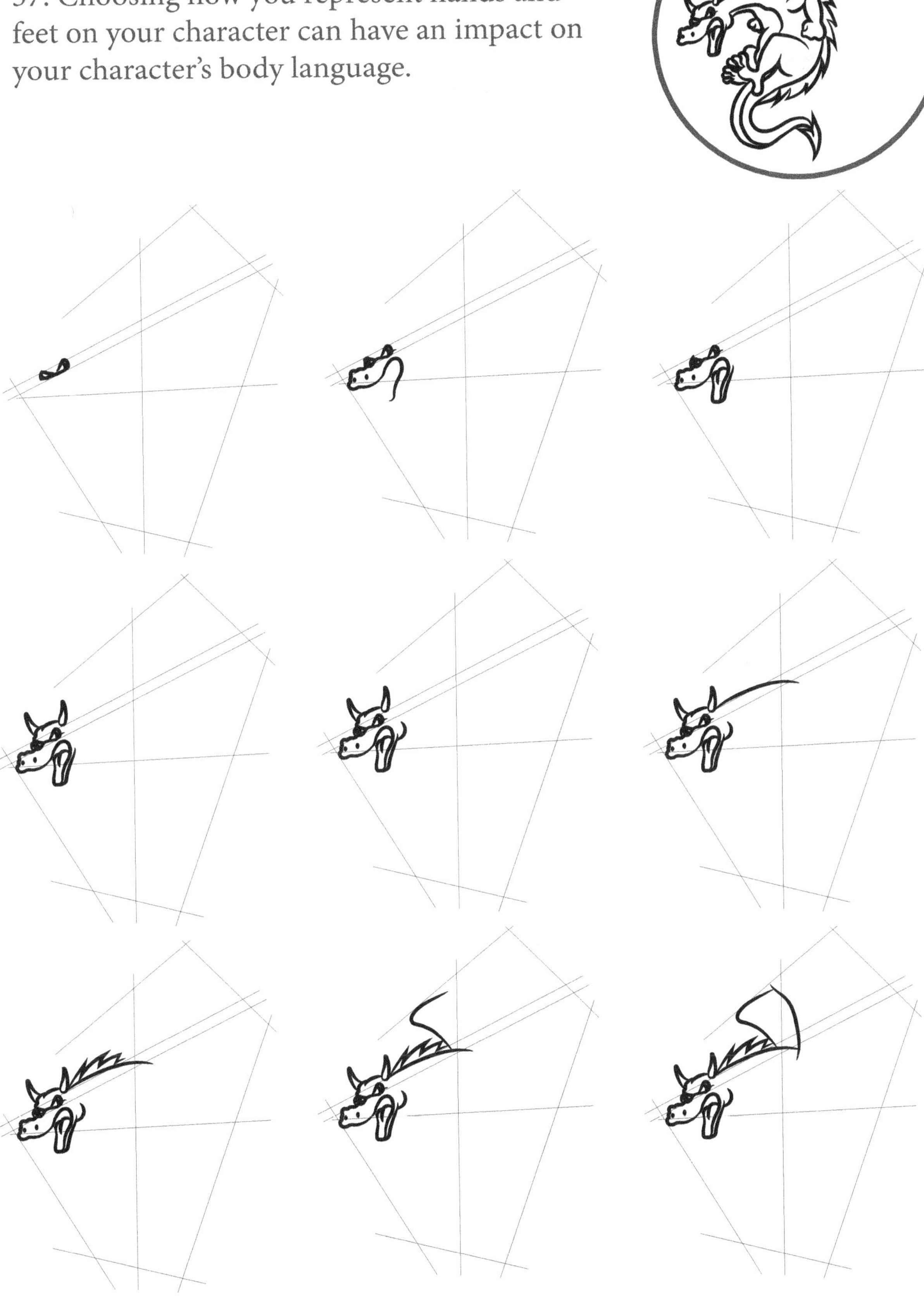

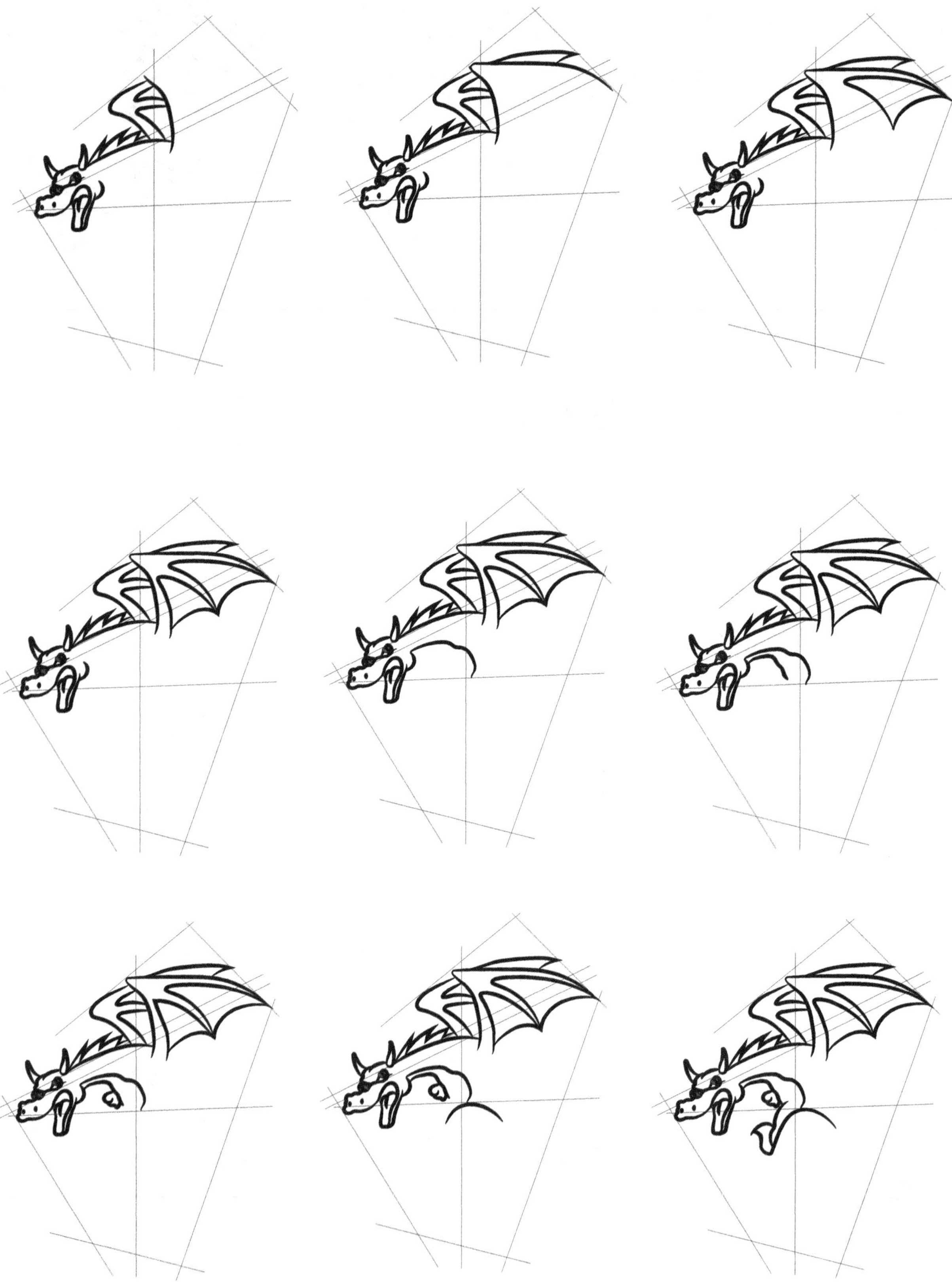

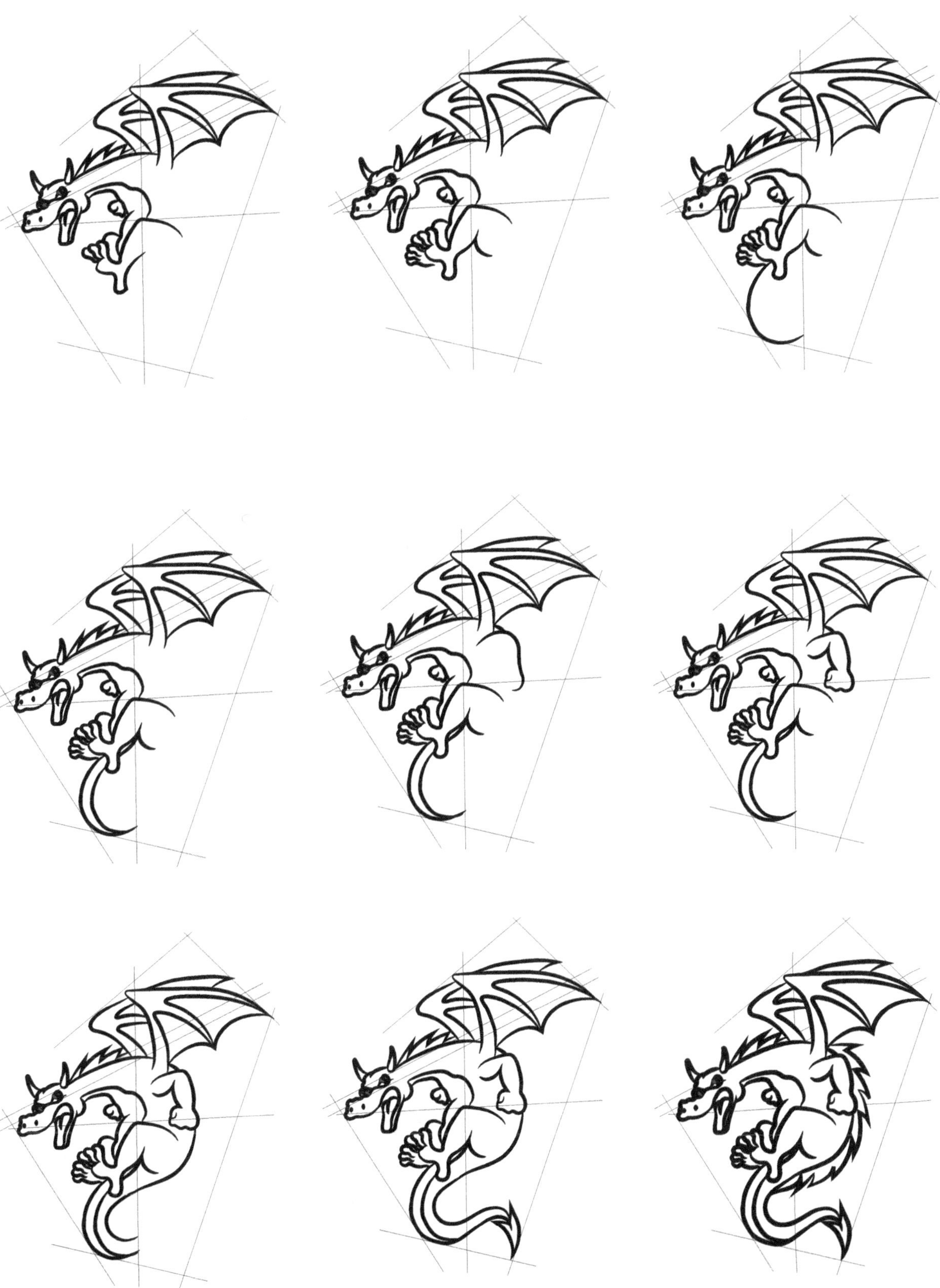

In Chinese mythology, there are Dragon Kings who rule over the four seas and control water and weather.

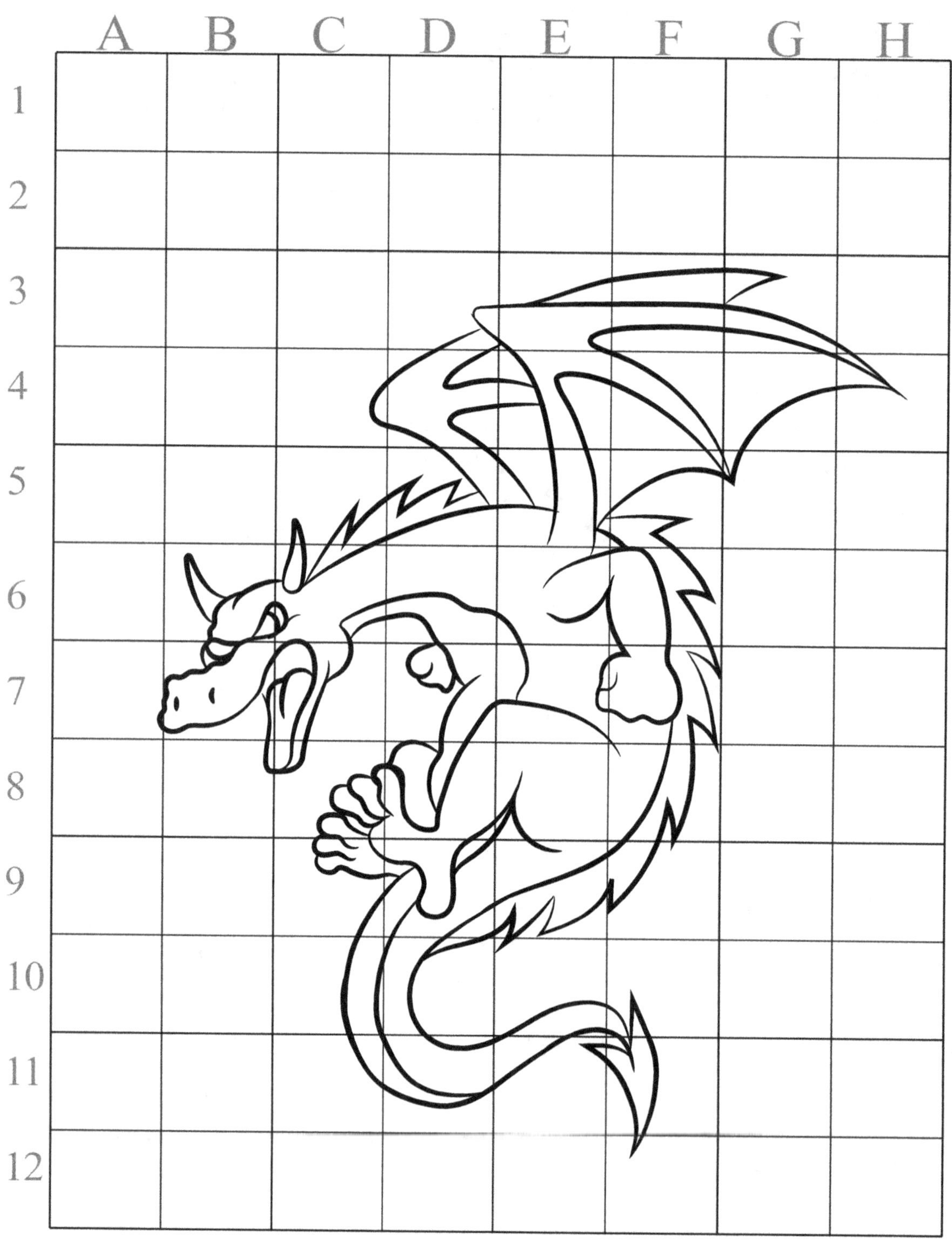

38. Use thinner lines to show greater detail for this character.

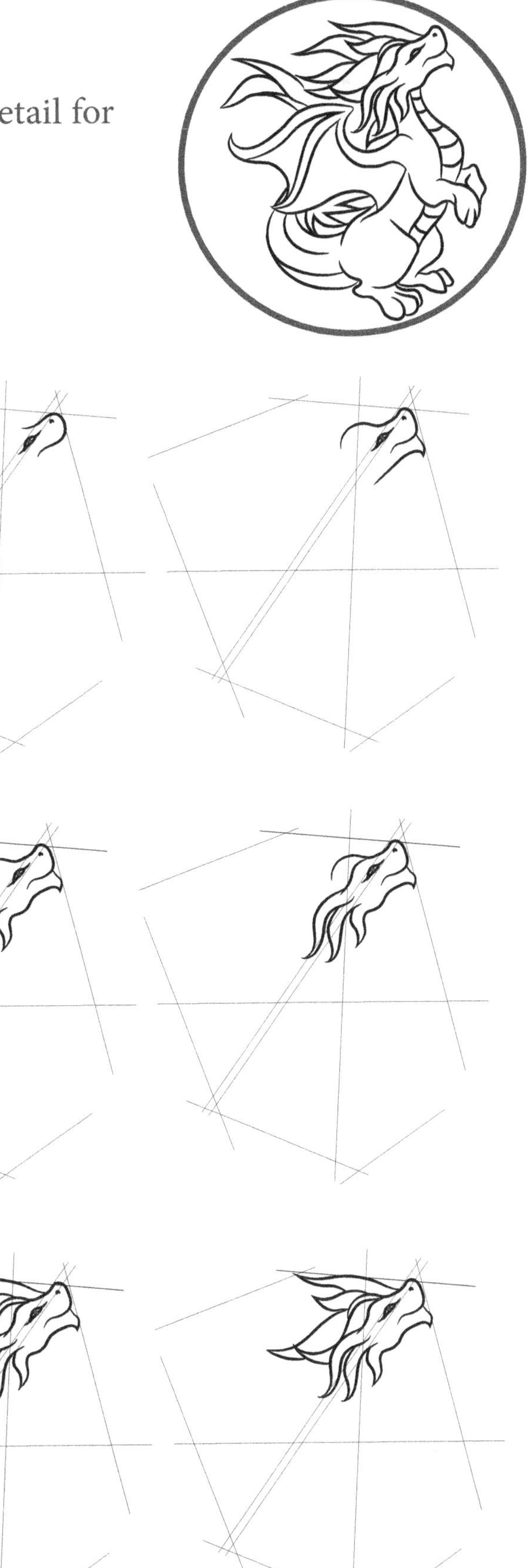

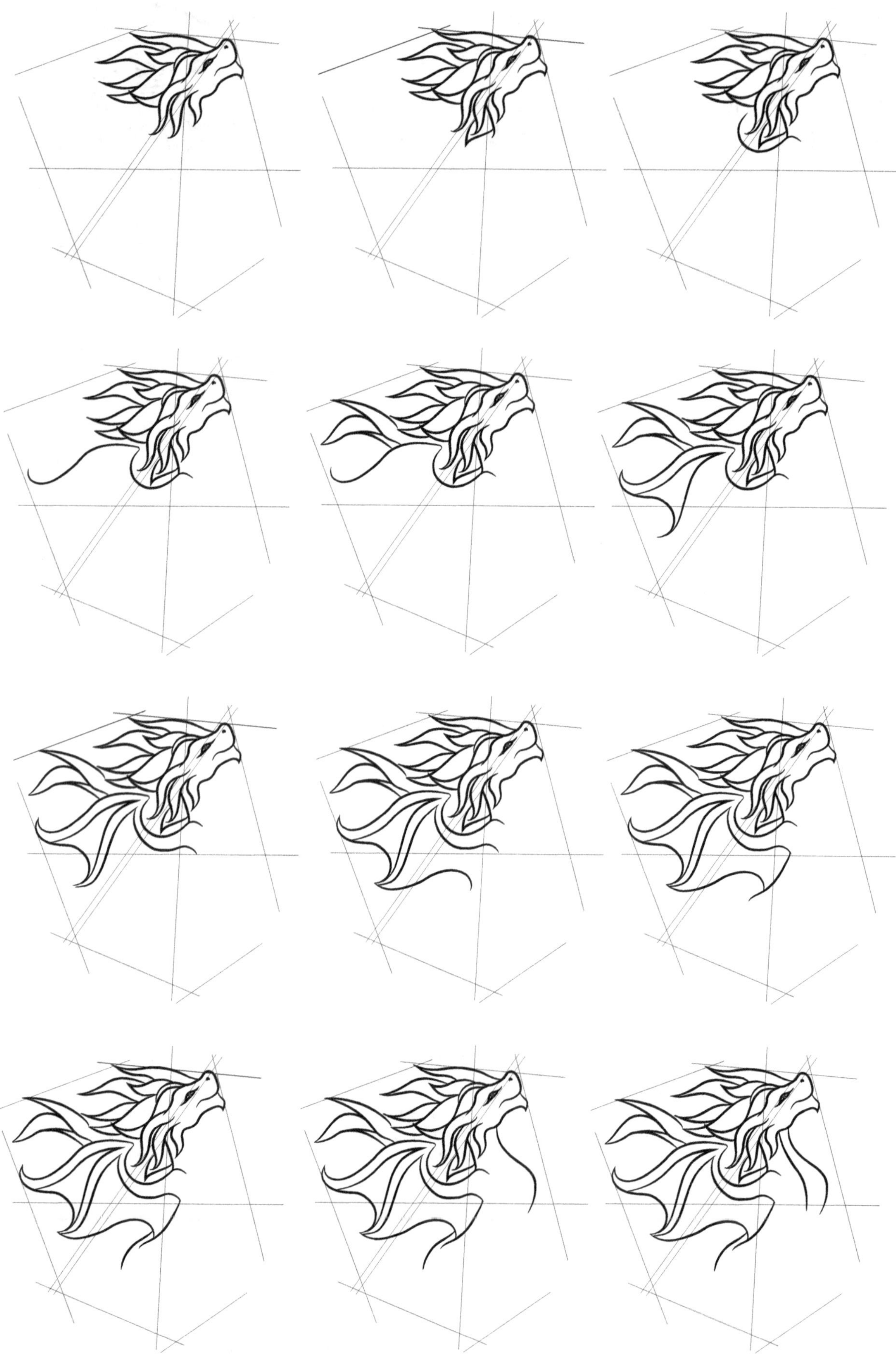

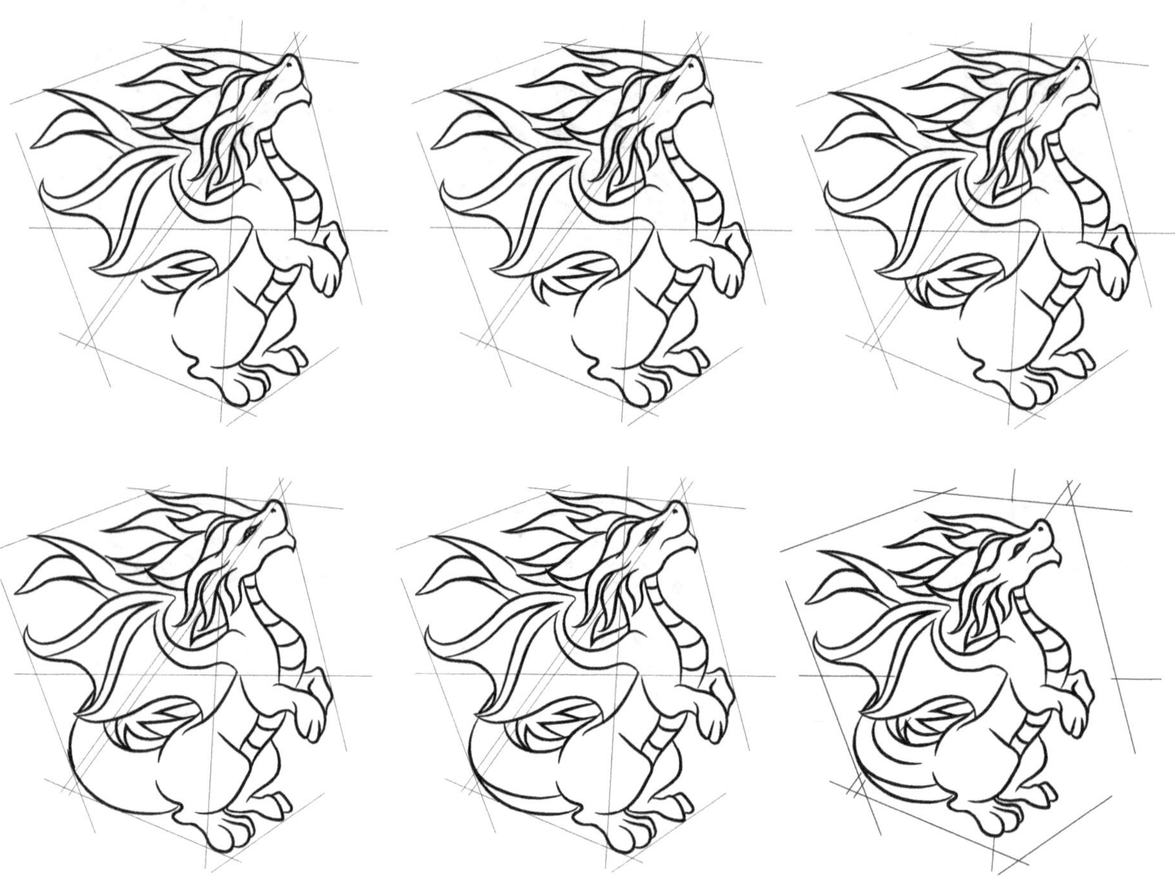

A distinguished dragon typically has an elegant and majestic appearance. Its scales are gleaming and meticulously detailed, often shimmering with iridescent colors.

39. You can change your character's features by making small adjustments.

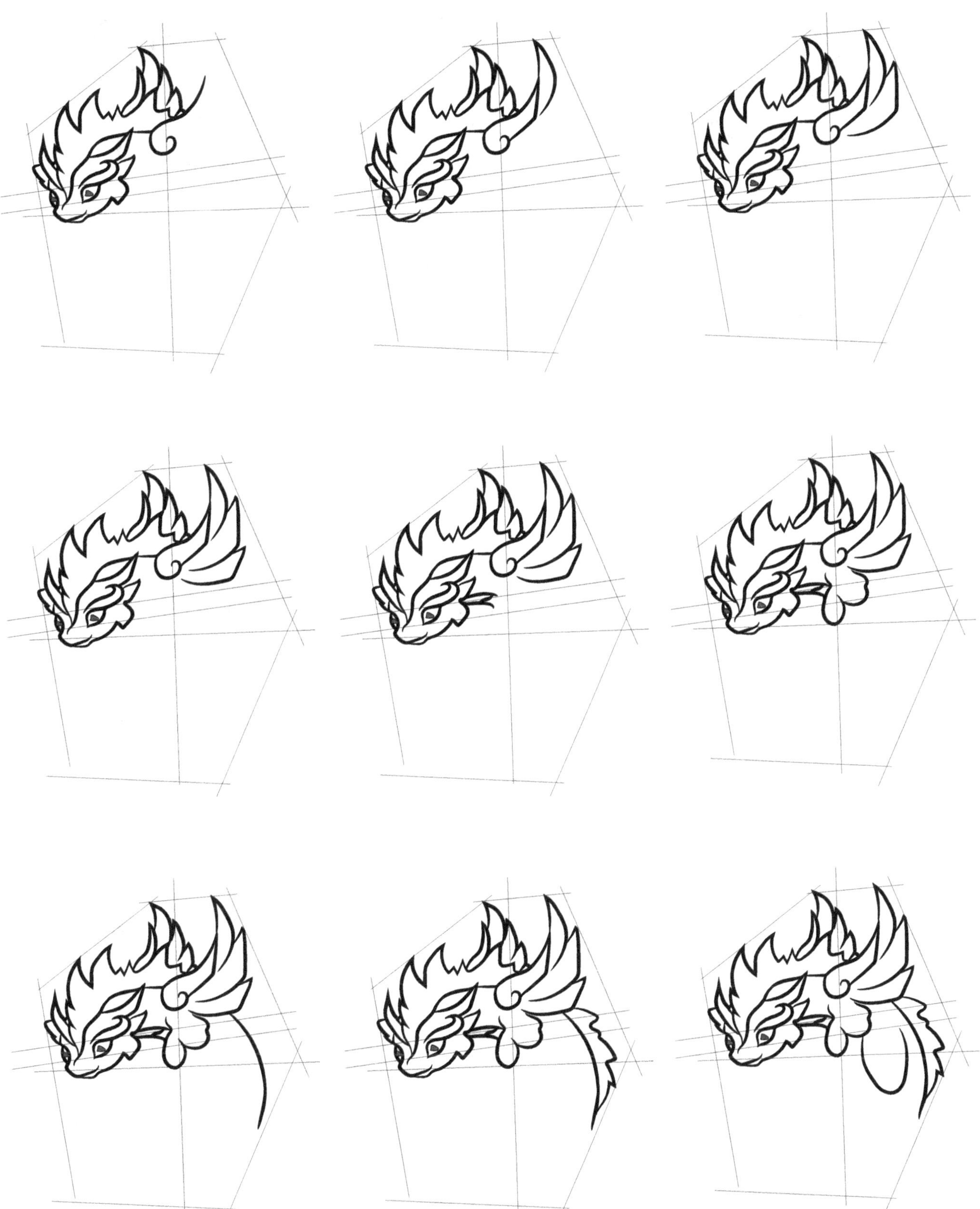

Dragons with big eyes are enchanting and often evoke a sense of
mystery, wisdom, and emotional depth. These dragons are a favorite in
various mythologies and fantasy stories due to their expressive and
captivating gaze.

40. Add flame to your
dragons mouth for
extra expression.

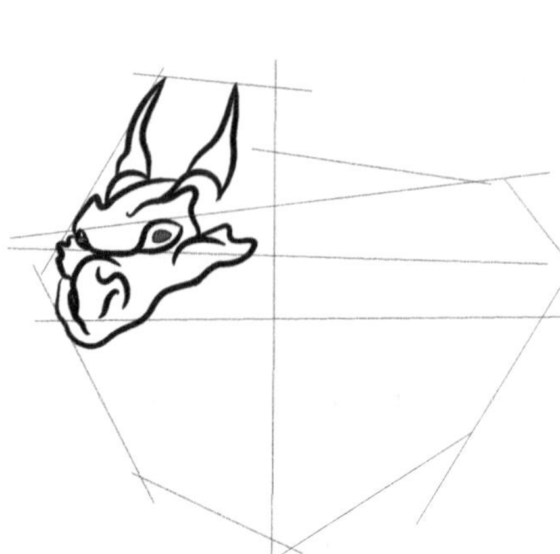

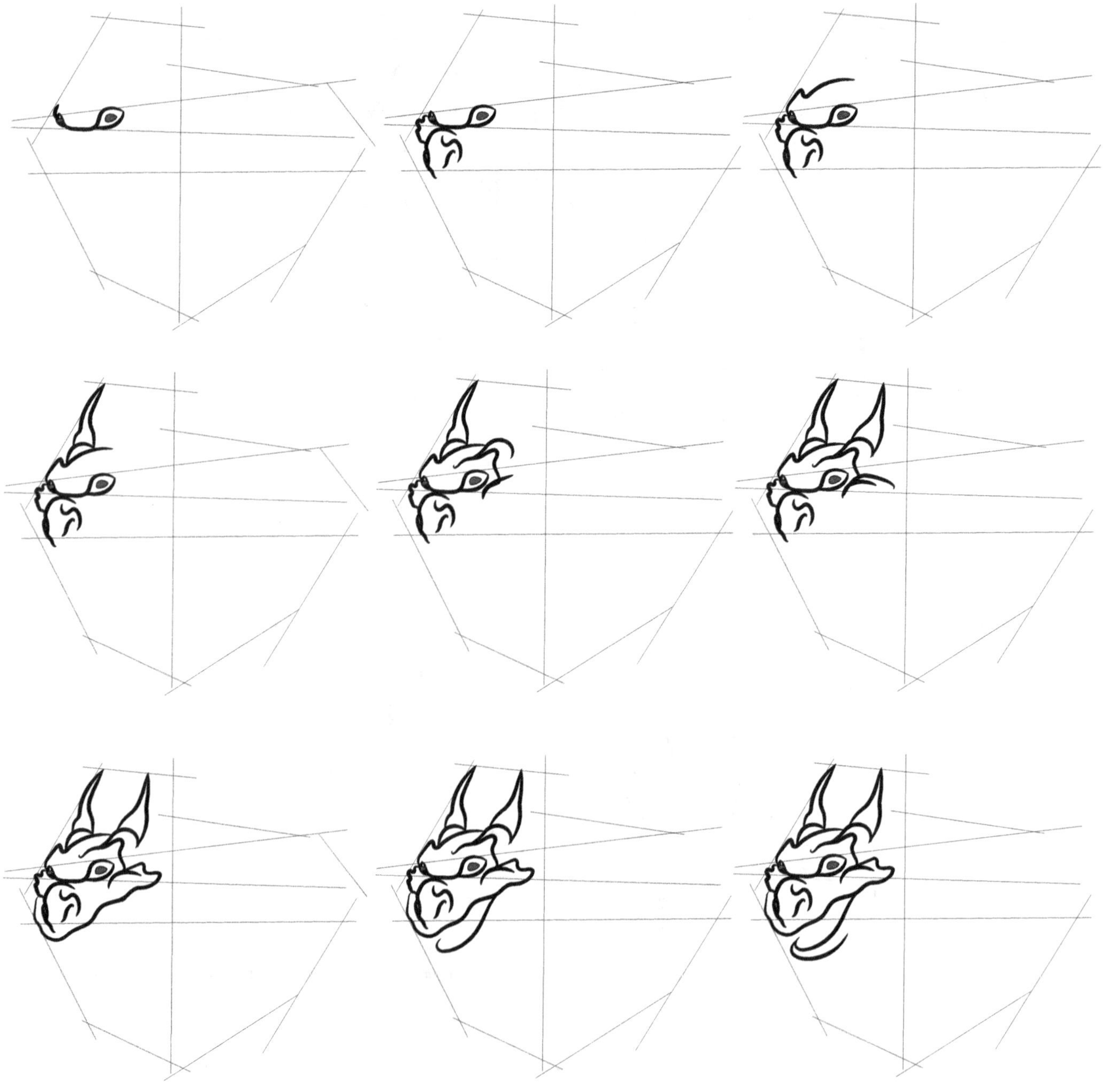

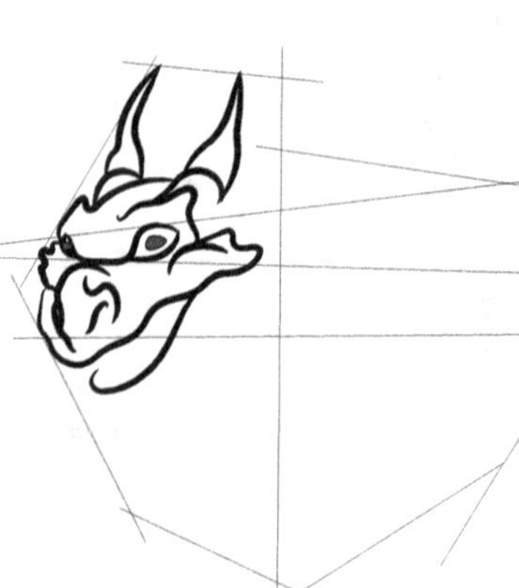

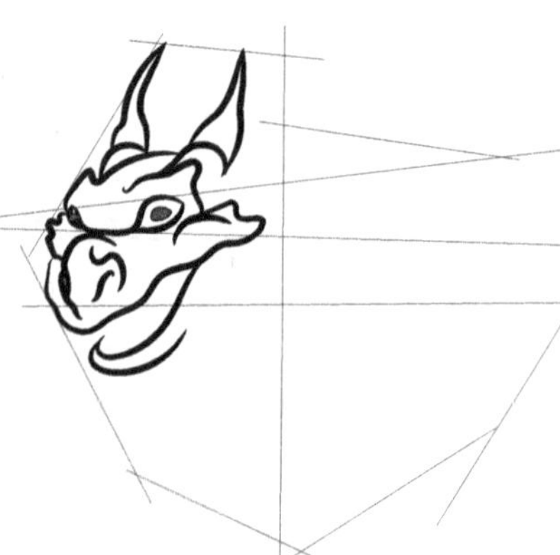

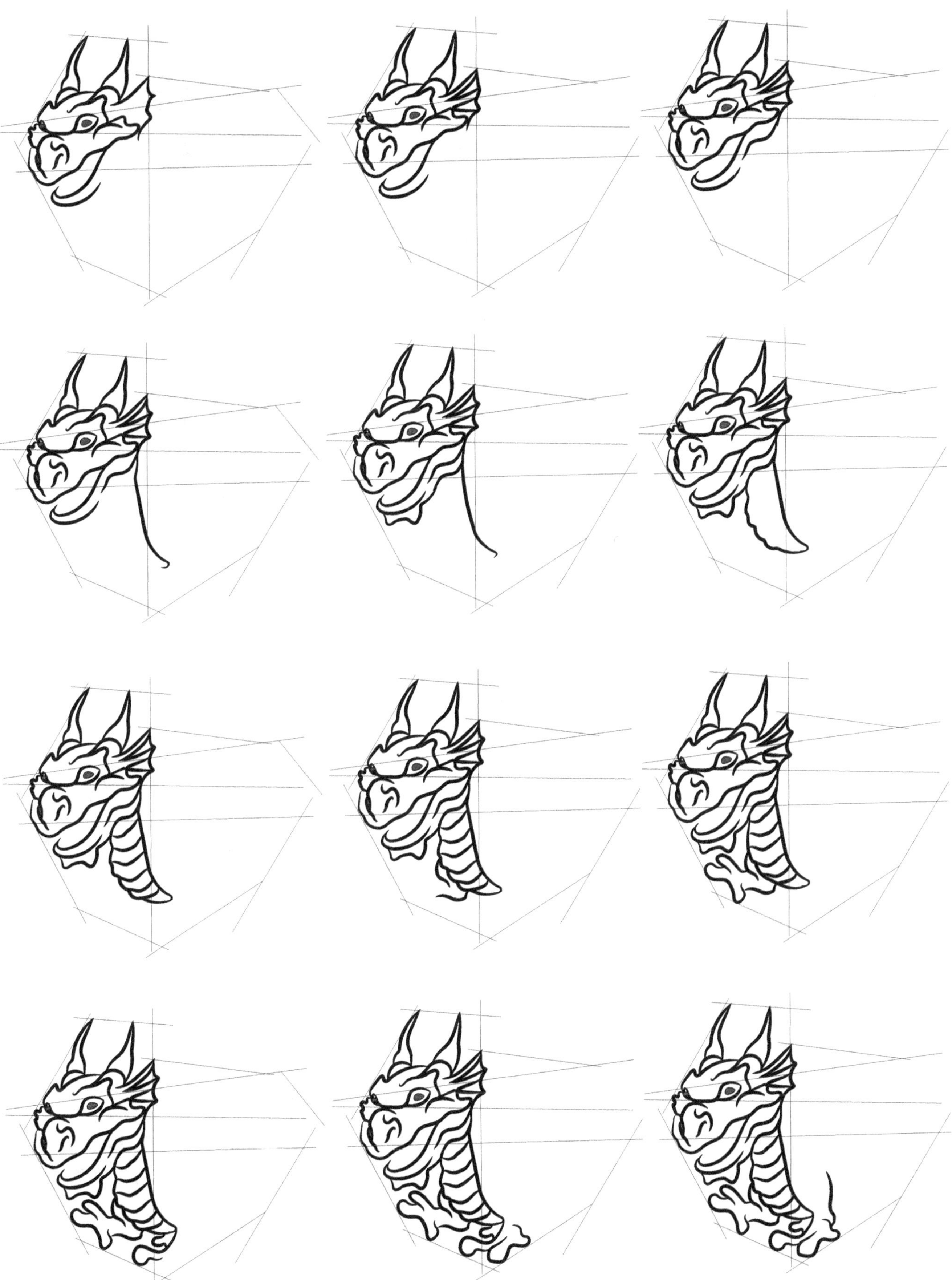

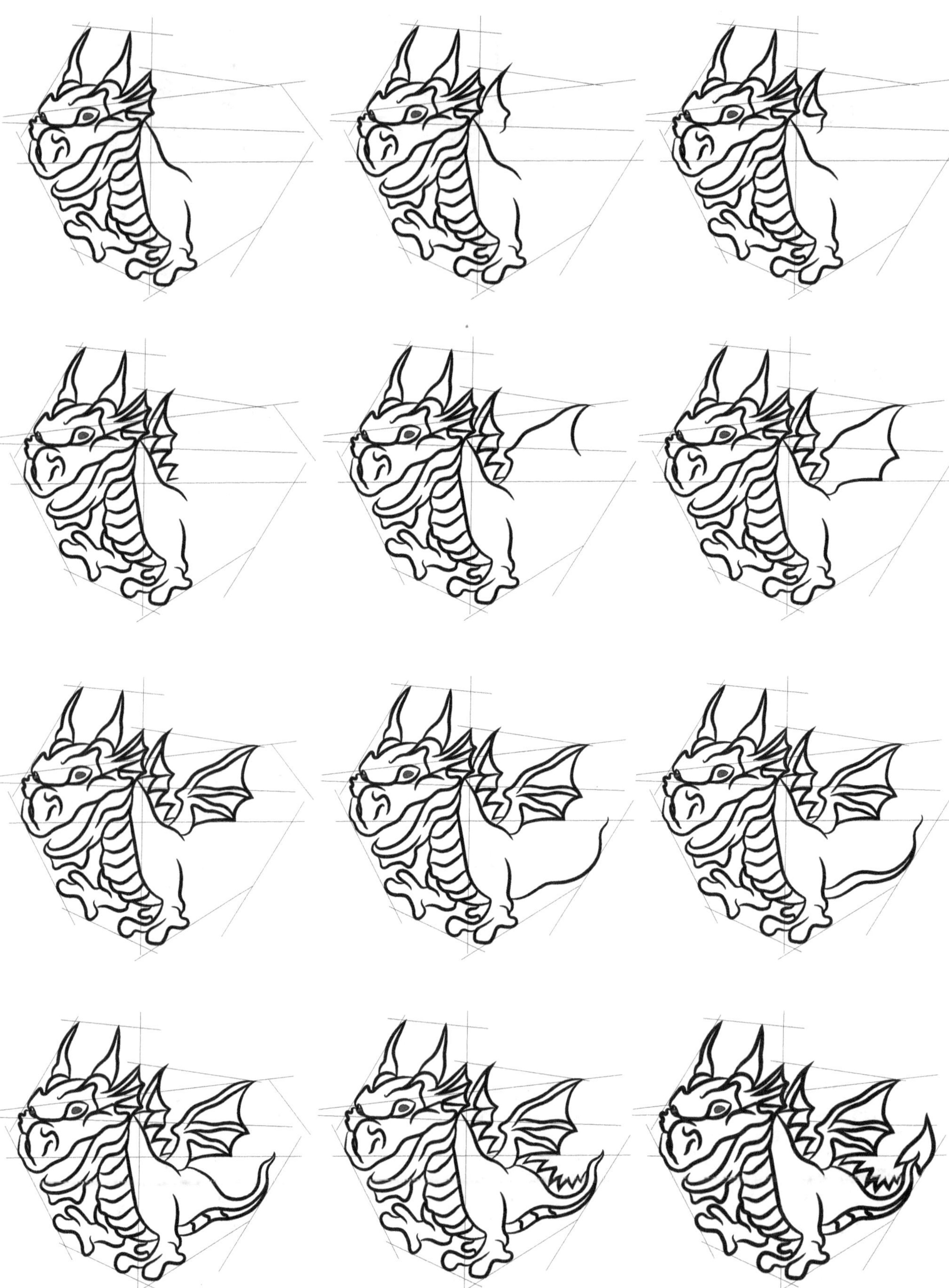

Flame-throwing dragons typically have powerful, muscular bodies covered in thick, armored scales that protect them from heat and attacks. Their heads are adorned with sharp horns, menacing teeth, and large, expressive eyes that can intimidate or mesmerize.

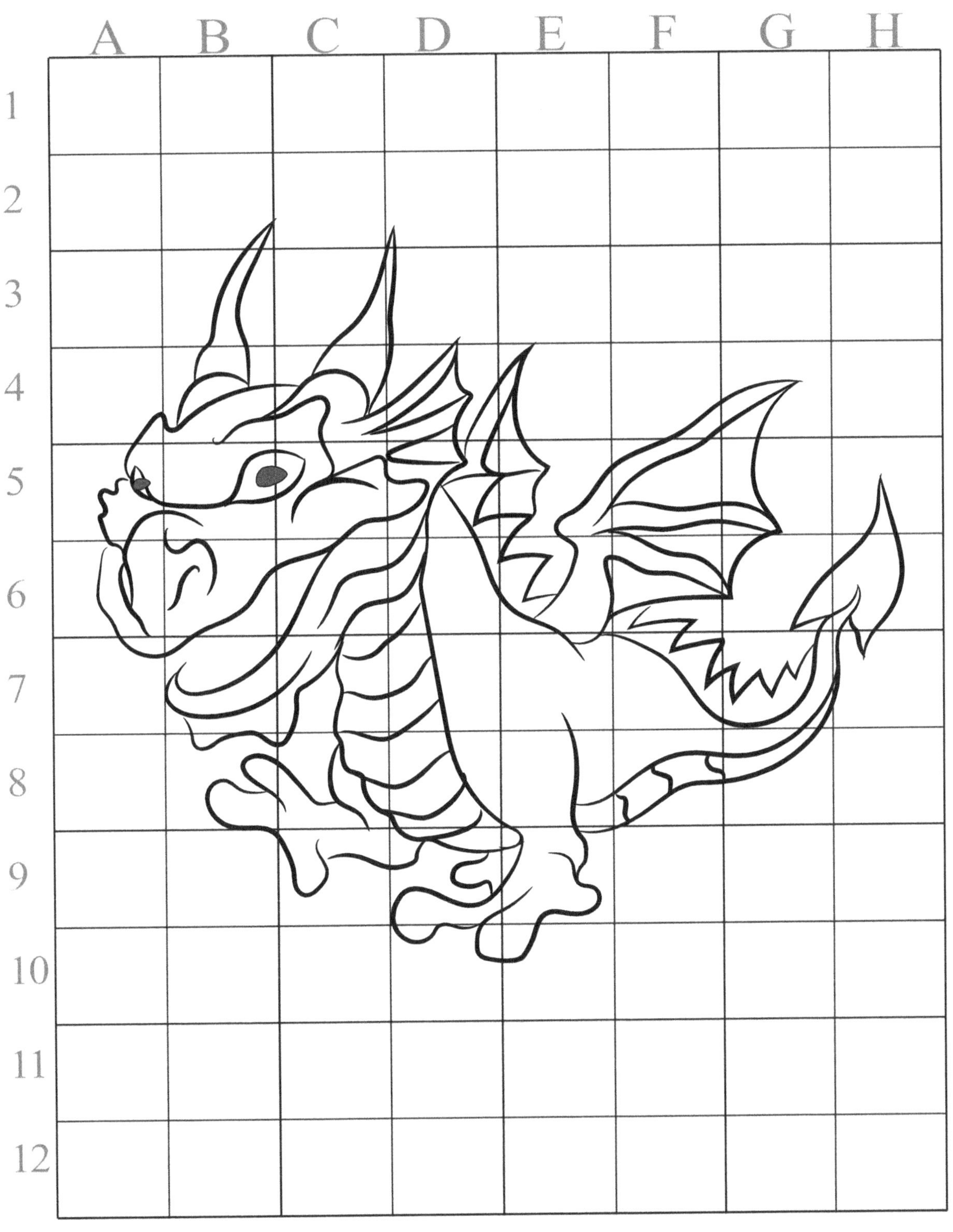